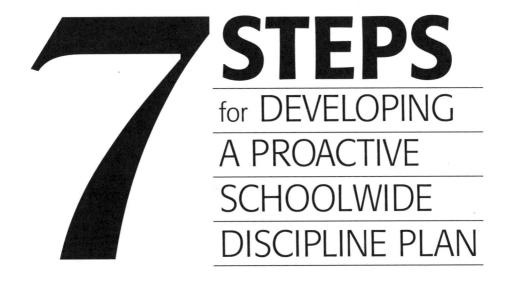

7 STEPS
for DEVELOPING
A PROACTIVE
SCHOOLWIDE
DISCIPLINE PLAN

Dedicated to my late sister-in-law, LeAnn Sinclair
(1948–2006)
Whose life personified these words of the writer Ralph W. Sockman:
"Nothing is so strong as gentleness and nothing is so gentle as real strength."

GEOFF COLVIN

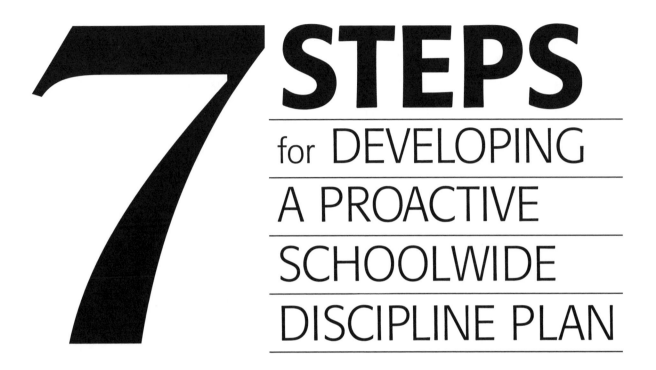

7 STEPS
for DEVELOPING
A PROACTIVE
SCHOOLWIDE
DISCIPLINE PLAN

A Guide for Principals and Leadership Teams

Foreword by George Sugai

CORWIN PRESS
A SAGE Publications Company
Thousand Oaks, CA 91320

For information:

Corwin Press
A Sage Publications Company
2455 Teller Road
Thousand Oaks, California 91320
www.corwinpress.com

Sage Publications Ltd.
1 Oliver's Yard
55 City Road
London EC1Y 1SP
United Kingdom

Sage Publications India Pvt Ltd
B 1/I 1 Mohan Cooperative
   Industrial Area
Mathura Road, New Delhi 110 044
India

Sage Publications Asia-Pacific Pte Ltd
33 Pekin Street #02-01
Far East Square
Singapore 048763

Printed in the United States of America

Library of Congress Cataloging-in-Publication Data

Colvin, Geoffrey, 1941-
7 steps for developing a proactive schoolwide discipline plan: A guide for principals and leadership teams / Geoff Colvin.
       p. cm.
Includes bibliographical references and index.
ISBN 978-1-4129-5097-8 (cloth)
ISBN 978-1-4129-5098-5 (pbk.)
    1. School discipline—United States. 2. School improvement programs—United States.
I. Title. II. Title: Seven steps for developing a proactive schoolwide discipline plan.

LB3012.2.C65 2007
371.50973—dc22

                                2006101267

This book is printed on acid-free paper.

09   10   11   10   9   8   7   6   5   4   3

Acquisitions Editor:	Allyson P. Sharp
Editorial Assistant:	Nadia Kashper
Production Editor:	Libby Larson
Copy Editor:	Julie Gwin
Typesetter:	C&M Digitals (P) Ltd.
Proofreader:	Dorothy Hoffman
Indexer:	Michael Ferreira
Cover Designer:	Michael Dubowe
Graphic Designer:	Lisa Riley

Contents

Foreword

I first met Geoff Colvin in the early 1980s when he was successfully educating students with serious emotional and behavioral disorders. At that time, Geoff was well known for his successful application of effective direct instruction and behavior analytic practices and principles to the management of problem social behavior. Geoff efficiently translated the research and guidance of Zig Engelmann, Doug Carnine, Rob Horner, Hill Walker, and many others so that real implementers could understand and successfully apply the most effective practices in real places with children and adults with significant learning and behavior challenges. One of Geoff's unique and most important strengths is his emphasis on the assessment and organization of the learning and teaching context. His goal always has been to design learning and teaching environments in which students and teachers can't help but be successful. This emphasis has applications (a) for the individual students, classrooms, and whole schools; (b) in preschool, elementary, middle, and high schools; and (c) in schools, families, community programs, alternative programs, and mental health and juvenile justice settings.

Although Geoff is one of the best at supporting the needs of students with severe problem behaviors, he also is well known for his work with whole classrooms, schools, and districts. True to his best practices approach, in this book, he has organized and applied systems and organizational change strategies to enable schools to identify, adopt, adapt, establish, and maintain effective behavior management practices for all students and staff members. Using his vast array of school and classroom experiences, this book is Geoff's comprehensive presentation of the "what's," "why's," and "how's" of effective schoolwide discipline. The purpose of this foreword is to highlight some of the key elements and features that make the contents of this book unique, important, and implementable.

RATIONALE ■

Geoff acknowledges that establishing an overall positive school climate is important so teaching will be uninterrupted, students will feel safe and be well behaved, teachers will be effective, academic achievement will be enhanced, and so forth. More important, however, he also explains how proactive schoolwide discipline is needed so the development of problem behavior can be prevented, resources can be used more effectively and efficiently, students with the most intensive learning and social behavior challenges can be assessed and supported, and staff members have predictable and dependable ways of addressing behavioral challenges at the schoolwide level. Understanding these reasons why proactive schoolwide discipline is important will give principals and leadership teams what they need to secure implementation agreements, commitments, and participation by staff members.

■ USER

Geoff makes an important statement in this book by overtly targeting principals and schoolwide implementation leadership teams. The contents of proactive schoolwide discipline must be understood, seen in real implementation contexts, practiced repeatedly with regular corrective and positive feedback, and modified based on outcome data. To achieve these outcomes, Geoff emphasizes that administrators must be active participants and leaders, for example, (a) making improvement of school discipline one of the school's top three improvement goals, (b) redirecting existing resources (e.g., staff development days, agenda items, supplies) to implementation of proactive school discipline, (c) participating in and enforcing implementation of practices and systems, (d) prompting and acknowledging staff participation, (e) modeling expected behavior, and so forth.

Geoff also emphasizes that changing staff routines and practices will require more than a series of professional development days in which staff members are told or they read about what they need to do to improve their classroom and behavior management practices. Instead, Geoff targets school leadership teams as the main mechanism by which intervention and organizational change is promoted and indicates that staff members from classroom and nonclassroom contexts formally and actively must be included: cafeteria and office staff, custodians, security personnel, playground and bus-loading supervisors, family and community members, and students. This team is a logical first choice for enhancing adoption of proactive schoolwide discipline practices because members represent the larger staff, know the culture of the school, and have daily access to the operations of the school. Most important, the team develops local behavioral capacity for sustained implementation.

■ THEMES

Geoff has included in this book a full range of effective behavior and classroom management practices and schoolwide discipline systems. More important are the themes that hold these interventions and practices together in a comprehensive and logical schoolwide organization. First, Geoff reminds us that an essential prerequisite to good behavior and classroom management is good instruction, defined as good curriculum, well-designed instruction, and effective and efficient presentation. Engaging instruction that results in high rates of successful learning is one of our most powerful behavior management tools. Geoff says it best: "Give students a reason to behave!"

Second, Geoff acknowledges the importance of having a clear and effective continuum of consequences for rule violations; however, he stresses that a comprehensive and formal approach to prevention is a necessity for a successful schoolwide discipline plan. Much of this book is about assessing the conditions under which both appropriate and inappropriate behaviors are likely to occur so strategies are put in place to (a) remove the triggers of problem behavior, (b) add the triggers of prosocial behavior, (c) teach prosocial replacement behaviors that work better or as well as inappropriate behaviors, (d) add reinforcers for desirable and expected behaviors that are more powerful than the reinforcers that maintain problem behaviors, and (e) remove the reinforcers that maintain existing problem behaviors.

Third, the problem behavior of individual students is often an immediate concern for educators; however, Geoff helps us understand the importance of establishing effective whole-school prosocial discipline plans to enhance the quality of supports for individual students. Whole-school approaches establish predictable environments in which all students and staff across all settings know what is expected of them and in which prosocial behaviors are promoted. When these proactive "host environments" are established, more attention can be focused with high quality on the needs of those students with intensive behavioral needs.

Fourth, the impact of even the most effective interventions will not be realized if those implementing those interventions are not fluent with the practice and aren't supported in its use. Thus, throughout this book, Geoff emphasizes systems factors that affect the adoption and sustained use of effective practices, for example, active principal support, leadership team coordination and implementation, data-based decision making, continuous progress monitoring, and so forth. If educators don't implement effective practices with high accuracy and consistency over time, maximum student benefits are not likely to be realized and sustained.

Finally, in all sections of this book, Geoff stresses that social behaviors can be taught, learned, maintained, and so forth in the same way as academic skills and concepts. Although it is widely accepted that academic behaviors are taught and retaught if errors occur, the misconception is that problem behaviors should be punished so that the student will "learn" that more appropriate behaviors should be displayed. Geoff stresses that students don't learn and aren't encouraged to display social behaviors through punishment. Instead, academic and social behaviors need to be taught, practiced, and encouraged through direct instruction and high rates of effective positive reinforcement, and, likewise, academic and social behavior errors (problems) should trigger completion of an error analysis to determine mis-rules and how to reteach correct responses.

RECOMMENDATIONS   ■

Although it might be easy to focus on the interventions and practices included in this book, I encourage users to keep Geoff's themes in mind to maximize understanding and implementation of their proactive school-wide discipline plan. In addition, users should consider the following implementation recommendations:

1. Use Geoff's checklists to assess your local and immediate situation carefully and thoroughly and to prioritize what is in place and what needs to be improved.

2. Use Geoff's worksheets as a guide, not as a recipe, to improve the efficiency and effectiveness of the development of your discipline plan.

3. Work as a team to build local capacity and competence.

4. Precede all adoption and implementation efforts with securing staff commitments and agreements.

5. Contextualize your adoption and implementation to the unique features of your school and classrooms.

6. Use Geoff's examples to emphasize guiding principles and to identify the "general case."

7. Define in measurable terms what the outcomes of all action planning activities are, and assess progress toward these outcomes on a frequent and regular basis.

8. Use your data to improve the effectiveness of your interventions and systems.

—George Sugai, PhD
Professor and Neag Endowed Chair
University of Connecticut
Neag School of Education
249 Glenbrook Road, Unit 2064
Storrs, CT 06269-2064

Acknowledgments

First and foremost, I wish to acknowledge my colleagues, George Sugai and Ed Kame'enui, for their pioneering work in Project PREPARE, a five-year, federally funded project at the University of Oregon. In this project, we developed and field tested a proactive model for schoolwide discipline and conducted research on its implementation. This model is essentially the cornerstone for this book.

George and his colleagues have expanded this model for implementation at national and international levels. They have provided very convincing results of what can be accomplished in schools and districts in developing positive behavior support programs for all students. George's work has touched hundreds of schools in the United States, Canada, and Australia. Similarly, Ed has provided very significant leadership in assisting schools to address literacy issues and has been particularly instrumental in raising reading scores through effective professional development from policy making to hands-on reading instruction. He, too, has made a powerful impact throughout American schools and schools abroad.

Second, I wish to acknowledge Patricia McRae, executive director of elementary education for Anchorage School District, Anchorage, Alaska. Patricia has worked very closely with me over a six-year period in implementing and maintaining, in almost 60 elementary schools and some secondary schools, the proactive approach to schoolwide discipline described in this book. Many of the details, applications, exemplars, and data portrayed in this book were derived from this alliance with Anchorage School District. Moreover, in conjunction with these efforts, Patricia has exercised very effective leadership in helping these schools raise achievement scores of their students.

Finally, I wish to acknowledge the very helpful collaboration from Carl Cole and Drew Braun of Bethel School District, Eugene, Oregon. Carl and Drew provided many opportunities, support, and feedback for me to address some of the finer details described in this book. Moreover, they have provided strong leadership and documentation showing the link between an effective schoolwide discipline plan and academic performance gains for its students. The Bethel Reading Project, through their leadership, has become a national model for addressing literacy issues with younger students.

Corwin Press would like to thank the following reviewers:

Cynthia M. Anderson
Associate Professor
School Psychology
University of Oregon
Eugene, OR

Craig Knotts
Charter School Administrator
Celerity Nascent Charter School
Los Angeles, CA

Stacey Neuharth-Pritchett
Associate Professor, Educational Psychology
The University of Georgia
Athens, GA

Susan Okeson
Principal
Chugiak Elementary School
Anchorage School District
Anchorage, AK

About the Author

 **Dr. Geoff Colvin** draws on his experience as a classroom teacher, in both special and general education, and as a school administrator, behavior consultant, and research associate at the University of Oregon.

He is a nationally recognized educational consultant who has assisted personnel in more than 200 school districts and agencies, nationally and internationally, on the subject of managing problem behavior, teaching challenging students, and school safety planning. He has authored and coauthored more than 80 publications, including the very popular book *Managing the Cycle of Acting-out Behavior in the Classroom* (2004) and the 2000 Telly Award winning video program, "Defusing Anger and Aggression."

As an administrator, he directed a juvenile detention school for five years and was the principal of a countywide school for seriously emotionally disturbed youth for five years. He served as the supervisor of special programs with Bethel School District, Eugene, Oregon, for several years, where he still serves as a consultant.

Dr. Colvin has a very special skill in being able to translate theory into practice. He is able to present clear explanations and analyses of learning and behavior and at the same time offer concrete examples with hands-on illustrations. He has a very strong, insightful understanding of the relationship between quality instruction and behavior management. His extensive knowledge and experience base, lively speaking style, and keen sense of humor have made him a highly sought-after speaker at national and international conferences.

Presently, he serves as a national educational and behavioral consultant.

Introduction

School discipline has always been perceived as essential for the proper functioning of a public school. There is a universal expectation that discipline is necessary for students to learn and that educators are expected to establish and maintain well-disciplined schools. The "public trust" is very clear—children's learning must be conducted in a safe and orderly environment. Moreover, discipline has been viewed for many generations as a goal in itself, that is, an important goal in education is to teach discipline to the students. Parents, community members, and educators historically have taken pride in maintaining well-disciplined schools. However, there has been a growing concern that the prevalence of problem behavior or the lack of school discipline is reaching crisis proportions. On school campuses, there are incidents of serious problem behavior related to safety. Homicides, assaults, rapes, drug activity, and crime in general are increasing. These concerns have arisen despite significant efforts to improve security by increasing the law enforcement presence on campuses, hiring security staff, attending to safe school design, and providing educational programs to address school safety. Gallup Polls of community members and educators for the past several years have ranked school discipline and student behavior in the top three major concerns facing our schools (Rose & Gallup, 1998, 2006).

Although there is general consensus on the problems facing our schools regarding school discipline, there is considerable variability and debate on the way these problems need to be addressed. Central to the issue is the role and value of punishment in changing behavior. Traditional methods are focused more on punishment procedures such as denying privileges, using corporal punishment, and excluding students from general educational settings. The basic approach has been "Spare the rod, spoil the child." In a sense, the expectation was that the students should do what is required, and if they choose otherwise, punishment would follow. Cooperation in school was expected and problem behavior was punished. Consequently, in this school of thought, the primary remedy for addressing problem behavior lies in increasing punitive measures. In effect, this approach proclaims "zero tolerance" for serious behavior, or "Get rid of the rotten apple."

More recently, educators have found that positive incentives, in conjunction with the traditional punitive procedures, have enhanced students' behavior and contributed significantly to establishing positive school climates. This school of thought recommends increasing the positive aspects in the discipline plan, specifically to systematically provide positive consequences for occurrences of desirable behavior. In effect, "Give students a reason to behave."

Several educators have pointed out some problems with this approach. Specifically, that some students will behave appropriately only if the external reinforcers are present. In other words, they will not develop intrinsic motivation.

However, there is strong documentation that shows significant behavior change can occur in school and classroom settings when a combination of positive and negative consequences are consistently applied contingent on desirable and undesirable behavior respectively. Nevertheless, there exists a major limitation in both these positive and negative approaches, applied either separately or in combination, and that is that they are essentially reactive in nature. They are consequences to be implemented after behavior has occurred. Negative measures follow problem behavior, and positive consequences follow expected behavior. The limitation arises because the procedures are contingent on the occurrence of either appropriate or inappropriate behavior.

There have been widespread efforts in public schools to take steps to prevent problem behavior before it has a chance to emerge and to focus on encouraging desirable behavior. The proactive approach, in contrast to reactive approaches, has been designed to create the kind of school environment that fosters desirable behavior and discourages problem behavior.

In the early 1990s, a research project based at the University of Oregon, Project PREPARE, developed and implemented a new model for managing problem behavior (Colvin, Kame'enui, & Sugai, 1993; Sugai, Kame'enui, & Colvin, 1990). This model combined the proactive features for developing a supportive school climate in conjunction with positive procedures for reinforcing desirable behavior and negative consequences for discouraging problem behavior.

This approach has been substantially expanded and implemented on a national and international scale (Sugai & Horner, 2002; Todd, Horner, Sugai, & Colvin, 1999; Turnbull et al., 2002). The Web site for the Center on Positive Behavioral Interventions and Supports, at the University of Oregon, www.pbis.org, provides a comprehensive body of literature and research on this approach.

In effect, this proactive approach, in conjunction with a balanced use of traditional practices for correcting the full range of problem behavior, offers a powerful tool for schoolwide discipline. In addition, these proactive measures help to establish the kind of school environment necessary for accomplishing the teaching and learning mission in schools.

Perhaps the best way of understanding the approach used in this book is to compare and contrast scenarios that occurred in two middle schools. The setting is the transition from the end of the first period to the beginning of the second period. The events in each school are described in Box 1 and Box 2, Sapphire Middle School and Emerald Middle School, respectively.

It is very clear that the scenario in Box 2, Emerald School, is far more desirable than the scenario in Sapphire School because the students leave in an orderly and focused manner, and there is very little downtime in the next period before the teacher is under way teaching math. By contrast, the students leave the classroom in Sapphire School (Box 1) in a rushed manner, there is more chaos in the hallways, and the receiving teacher has to struggle to get the students settled down and working on math.

Box 1: Transition From First to Second Period in Sapphire Middle School	Box 2: Transition From First to Second Period in Emerald Middle School
The teacher hurries with the announcements to close out the first period before the bell rings. When the bell rings, the students grab their books, converge on the door, and spill out into the hallway. There is much physical contact, and voices are raised. In the hallway, some students are standing in a group talking, others are heading to the next class, some are running or walking very quickly to race each other, and another group is engaged in a pushing match. A teacher passing by reprimands the students who are pushing and horsing around. There are obvious pencil and pen lines drawn on the walls. Then there is a mad rush to the next class by the bulk of the students to avoid being late. The receiving teacher is standing behind her desk urging the students to settle down and go to their desks quietly. After several minutes, the students are in their desks, and several are still talking to each other. The lesson begins with the teacher asking the students to cease talking and listen.	The teacher completes announcements to close out the lesson and then reminds the students of the expectations in the hallways to walk, talk quietly, and keep moving. The students proceed to the door in a reasonably orderly manner and walk to the next class chatting to each other on the way. A teacher passing by nods to some students and tells others to have a good day. The walls are clean and an attractive poster lists the school's hallway expectations. The receiving teacher is standing at the door just outside the classroom, greets the students, and thanks them for arriving so punctually to class. She then tells them to get started with the math problem that is on the overhead. The students begin working on the problem and talking ceases. The teacher quickly checks the initial entry problem and proceeds with the lesson for the day.

However, it was no accident that the students in Emerald School were behaving better than those at Sapphire School. There were substantial differences in the teachers' behavior in each school. In Emerald School, the teacher closed out the lesson in a timely manner and reminded the students of the expected behavior in the hallway, an eye-catching poster on the wall in the hallway also served as a reminder, a passing teacher initiated positive interactions with the students, the receiving teacher was outside the door to greet the students and acknowledge their punctuality, and she had an entry task on the overhead for the students to begin working on immediately. On the other hand, the teacher at Sapphire School was rushed at the end of the lesson, the passing teacher in the hallway had a negative interaction with the students, the hallway walls were somewhat disfigured with pencil and pen lines, and the receiving teacher was waiting behind the desk in the classroom for the students and had to ask them several times to go to their desks and quiet down.

In this example, the teachers at Emerald School provided an illustration of the operating details of a proactive approach to managing the transition between classes. This book is designed to fully describe the procedural details in developing, implementing, and maintaining a proactive schoolwide discipline plan.

The book is organized into two sections. Section I presents the critical perspectives of this book and the process details. Chapter 1 describes background information on specific concerns facing the public schools regarding discipline. Chapter 2 provides a review and analysis of traditional and current school discipline systems leading to the need for a proactive discipline plan. A brief critique is also provided on effective professional development practices. Chapter 3 presents an elaboration of the critical underpinning for the success of a schoolwide plan defining the role of administrative support, specifically the role of the principal. Details are provided highlighting concrete steps for the principal to take to ensure successful implementation. Chapter 4 describes a process for implementing a schoolwide plan through the agency of a school leadership team. The school leadership team is designed to provide a clear-cut process for ensuring reliable implementation of the plan by the entire faculty.

Section II provides detailed information on the content for the proactive schoolwide discipline team. There are seven components in the plan: (a) a purpose statement, (b) schoolwide behavior expectations, (c) teaching the behavior expectations, (d) maintaining the behavior expectations, (e) correcting problem behavior, (f) using the data, and (g) sustaining the plan for the long haul.

This book is also designed to enable school personnel to carefully evaluate what they already have in place in their school setting. Components that are already effective can then be included in the overall plan. While the book may have useful information for many service providers, it is designed for three groups of professionals in particular: (a) educators, including school administrators, regular and special education teachers, school psychologists, counselors, educational specialists, and classified staff; (b) professional development specialists at building, district, and state levels; and (c) personnel preparation providers, such as college professors, and preservice and inservice trainers and consultants.

The reader is referred to an appendix section at the back of the book. This section contains all of the checklists, forms, and plans presented throughout the book. These appendices may be reproduced or adapted for personal use in the classroom, school, or district.

Section I

Critical Perspectives

The primary purpose of this book is to provide educators with guidelines, procedures, and strategies for developing and implementing a proactive schoolwide discipline plan. However, before the specific steps are described, it is important for the reader to review several key perspectives that provide the foundation for the plan. This critical information is presented in the next four chapters: (a) establishing the need for a proactive discipline plan, (b) essential features of a proactive schoolwide discipline plan, (c) the vital role of the principal and administrative support, and (d) establishing a building leadership team.

1

Establishing the Need for a Proactive Discipline Plan

Although many topics related to education lead to discussion and debate, one seems indisputable—public schools are under incredible pressure today. School officials, educators, and students must respond to (a) ongoing concerns regarding school safety, violence, and bullying; (b) the increasing cultural and academic diversity of the student body; (c) the school drop-out crisis; (d) the growing presence and impact of special-needs students; (e) the demands arising from the No Child Left Behind Act to raise school achievement scores; and (f) issues of student alienation. There is no assumption that if schools paid more attention to positive approaches to schoolwide discipline, these pressures would be effectively solved. However, if an effective proactive schoolwide plan were to be established, these problems would be reduced, and more important, the stage would be set for schools to systematically address these challenges. These major challenges will be reviewed to highlight the need for an effective and efficient proactive schoolwide discipline plan as a necessary ingredient for addressing and helping to solve the problems.

■ ONGOING CONCERNS REGARDING SCHOOL SAFETY, VIOLENCE, AND BULLYING

School violence, more than any other topic, has galvanized public attention and concern. The Youth Violence Fact Sheet from the National Center for Injury Prevention and Control (2006) reported that school violence represents one of our society's chief public health concerns. Many observers have noted that violence seems endemic to our society (Duhon-Sells, 1995; Krug, Mercy, Dahlberg, & Zwi, 2002; Resnick, Ireland, & Borowsky, 2004; Walker, Colvin, & Ramsey, 1995) and that the spillover to schools is becoming alarmingly evident as per the most recent unspeakable shooting tragedies inflicted by students on staff and students in Arkansas, Mississippi, Kentucky, Minnesota, Oregon, and Colorado. Moreover, despite the intensive focus on making schools safer over the past several years, the National Center for Disease Control, in a national survey of trends in risk factors for violence in schools (carrying a weapon, carrying a gun, physical fighting, and being injured in fighting), showed no overall change in the period from 1991 to 2005. Public schools are far from being safe environments where educators and students can focus their attention and energies solely on teaching and learning.

Chapter 6 introduces the schoolwide behavior expectations, that is, behaviors required of all students in all school settings. Typically, one of these expectations is centered on school safety. For example, one behavior expectation could be (or should be), "Be safe." This focus, along with the teaching and maintenance of the expectations, Chapters 7 and 8 respectively, helps in a very significant manner to make schools safer.

■ THE INCREASING CULTURAL, LINGUISTIC, AND ACADEMIC DIVERSITY OF THE STUDENT BODY

Hodgkinson (1998) reported on the unique cultural and linguistic diversity changes at a worldwide level and in the student population in American schools. Using census data, he predicted that by the year 2010, whites will comprise only 9% of the world's population—the smallest ethnic minority—and that the number of ethnically and culturally diverse children in the United States will increase significantly. It was projected that while 26% of all Americans would be nonwhite, 36% of children would be nonwhite. The diversity of the school population is found not only in terms of ethnicity, but also in terms of social class and economic status. For example, the National Center for Children in Poverty (2006) reported that 18% of America's children are living in poverty today, showing an increase of 1.3 million since the year 2000. These very needy children bring to the school educational, social, and familial problems that schools are expected to overcome. The increase in cultural, linguistic, and economic diversity poses serious and substantial challenges for schools already faced with diminishing fiscal resources.

Again, cultural and linguistic diversity issues, especially acceptance and respect for one another, can be directly addressed through one of the behavioral expectations described in Chapter 6. For example, one behavior expectation could be (or should be), "Respect one another." This focus helps schools to develop a warm and welcoming climate where all students are respected and valued.

SCHOOL DROP-OUT CRISIS ■

Today, nearly all students are expected to graduate from high school. Yet hundreds of thousands of students in the United States leave school early each year without a diploma (National Center for Education Statistics, 2002). It appears that school drop-out rates are increasing. Barton (2005) found high school completion peaked at 77.1% in 1969 at the national level. By 2000, the completion rate had dropped to 69.9%, and the graduation rate continued to decrease to about 66% of the student population through 2004. The costs to individuals and society are very significant when students drop out of school. The number of students in our nation who are not completing school is particularly alarming in today's society because there are few employment opportunities that pay living wages and benefits for those who have neither completed a high school education nor acquired necessary basic skills. For example, Hall (2005) reported the unemployment rates for high school dropouts is 30% higher than that for graduates and that the dropouts who are employed earn 30% less than graduates. Moreover, students who do not complete school cost taxpayers billions of dollars in lost revenues, welfare, unemployment, crime prevention, and prosecution (Joint Economic Committee, 1991; National Center for Education Statistics, 1995, 2003).

Researchers have found lower rates of school drop-outs occur if there is a positive school climate, if a sense of belonging is fostered, and if systematic efforts are made to assist students to succeed in school (Lehr, Johnson, Bremer, Cosio, & Thompson, 2004). Clearly, a major goal in developing a proactive schoolwide climate is to create the kind of environment that fosters school success, which obviously will contribute to students staying in school and graduating.

EDUCATING STUDENTS WITH SPECIAL ■
NEEDS FOR BEHAVIORAL SUPPORTS

The challenge of managing discipline and providing adequate instruction in schools is further intensified by the growing presence of students identified with emotional and behavioral disorders and, in general, students with special needs. On average, students with disabilities are at greatest risk of dropping out of school. The drop-out rate for students with emotional or behavioral disabilities is approximately twice that of general-education students (Kaye, 1997; Wagner, 1995). Among youth with disabilities who drop out of school, the highest proportions are students with learning disabilities (32%) and students with emotional and behavioral disabilities (50%) (Wagner, 1991).

Of the 58% who did not graduate, 4% left school because they exceeded the age limit, 50% dropped out of school (twice the general population rate), and 4% were expelled. The graduation rate for students with disabilities and other student populations continues to be far below the national average. According to *OSERS 23rd Report to Congress* (2001), only 57% of youth with disabilities graduated with regular diplomas during the 1998–1999 school year. In addition, Lehr et al. (2004) reported other student populations who have disproportionately high rates of dropping out include those from low socioeconomic circumstances or single-parent families and those who are identified as Native American or Hispanic/Latino.

In this book, there is no claim that by developing a proactive school-wide discipline plan, students with disabilities or special needs will become successful. These students typically need carefully planned, indi-vidualized support (Horner, Sugai, Todd, & Lewis-Palmer, 2005). However, the claim is made that if a strong, supportive environment is established schoolwide, the staff associated with serving these students with special needs will be able to provide more effective services. In addition, as these services become more effective, the changes incurred will more likely be maintained in a strong, positive, and proactive school climate.

■ EFFECTIVELY IMPLEMENTING THE NO CHILD LEFT BEHIND ACT

The No Child Left Behind Act of 2001 has focused recent attention on the problem of school drop-outs and is driving efforts to increase graduation rates for all students. This law holds schools accountable for student progress using indicators of adequate yearly progress, including measures of academic performance and rates of school completion. Educators, administrators, and policymakers at district and state levels are in need of interventions that will increase high school graduation rates for all students, especially those at risk of school failure. With the recent empha-sis on accountability, personnel from local and state education agencies are charged with developing programs that engage students in school and learning, ensure acquisition of academic and social skills necessary for adulthood, and result in high rates of school completion (Lehr et al., 2004).

While an effective, proactive schoolwide discipline plan in and of itself will not necessarily raise school achievement scores, it sets the stage to enable more effective and efficient teaching to occur. In other words, the schoolwide plan helps to provide the necessary environment for teachers to address the requirements of the No Child Left Behind Act.

■ PREVENTING STUDENT ALIENATION

Student alienation with school has been identified as one of the major con-tributing factors for the unacceptable high rates of school drop-outs and occurrences of school violence (Jordan, Lara, & McPartland, 1996; McNeely, Nonnemaker, & Blum, 2002; Scanlon & Mellard, 2002). Interventions designed to address student alienation need to be implemented at many levels, such as redesigning curricula; providing appropriate academic and behavioral supports; providing ongoing, schoolwide professional development for the faculty; and integrating parental and community supports. Again, these systemic interventions will be more successful if school climate issues are effectively addressed by creating an environment in which all students and faculty are respected and valued. Developing a climate to support student alienation interventions is a primary goal of implementing and maintaining a proactive schoolwide discipline plan.

SUMMARY ■

Public schools are under incredible pressure. Dwindling resources, stressed-out staff, multiple demands, and greater numbers of special-needs children make the task of providing education more complex and more difficult. Educators must respond to students who are culturally and ethnically diverse. Hodgkinson (1998), in an analysis of census data, reported that the number of minority students was increasing annually and that the trend would likely continue through 2010. Similar trends can be seen in terms of economic status. For example, in 1993, more than 23% of school-age children in the United States were living below the poverty level. In addition to facing the challenges associated with cultural, linguistic, and economic diversity, public schools are dealing also with diminishing fiscal resources and extraordinary pressure to increase student achievement (Colvin, Kame'enui, & Sugai, 1993).

To face these challenging and almost overwhelming pressures, there are many levels that need to be addressed, including legislation; national, state, and community supports; law enforcement; service agencies; and parents. However, there remains the overriding assumption that public schools should be able to address the problems and develop effective and workable solutions. One dimension, for which the school is clearly responsible, is its capacity to establish a safe, nurturing, and positive environment that is designed to promote desirable behavior and to reduce and control problem behavior. There is a need to develop systems of support capable of serving all students. These systems of support have more chance of being successful if the school environment is set up to enable these interventions to be implemented and maintained. Establishing a positive, proactive schoolwide discipline plan is a necessary first step for enabling schools to achieve their goals and responsibilities.

2

Essential Features of a Proactive Schoolwide Discipline Plan

Colvin, Kame'enui, and Sugai (1993) presented a case for the need for public schools to approach school discipline in a different way. The argument was made that historically, school discipline was largely based on punitive and reactive measures. Essentially, rules were defined and violators were responded to with preordained negative consequences. Colvin et al. (1993) documented that this approach was quite inadequate based on the longstanding issues discipline paired with increased concerns regarding school safety, classroom disruption, and growing numbers of students dropping out of school or being suspended and expelled from school. A new model was developed with a highly explicit focus on proactive measures. In effect, the focus was to establish and increase the behaviors that enable students to be successful in school versus the prevailing models aimed at eliminating undesirable behaviors. With this emphasis, Colvin et al. (1993) developed an approach based on using the same instructional principles used for teaching academic skills for teaching expected behavior in school. In this way, desirable behavior was treated as a skill to be learned and taught in much the same way as academic skills. In effect, if desirable behaviors are to be established in a school, they need to be taught.

This instructionally based model was used as a prototype in Project PREPARE (Sugai, Kame'enui, & Colvin, 1990). Substantial gains were reported in improved behavior, reduction in office referrals for discipline, and significant reductions in suspensions and expulsions (Colvin et al., 1993). This model was implemented in inner city schools in Chicago; Fort Lauderdale; Portland, Oregon; and Los Angeles. In addition, the model was implemented successfully in rural areas including eastern Oregon; Veneta, Oregon; Washington State; and Iowa.

To support instruction in making learning effective and efficient for all students, a definable infrastructure needs to be firmly in place. The essential supporting elements in this infrastructure include an operational vision encompassing high student achievement, administrative support, research-based curricula, systematic ongoing professional development, adoption of effective instructional practices, and data management systems involving both formative and summative assessment. In successful schools, these features are carefully integrated to provide a systemic approach to instruction (Cotton, 1995; Togneri & Anderson, 2003).

To establish and sustain a proactive schoolwide discipline plan, a systemic approach composed of essential components needs to be fully used. These features will be briefly described: (a) primary focus, (b) systemic approach, (c) instructional approach, (d) a building leadership team-based approach, (e) a data-based decision-making process, (f) a continuum of positive behavior and academic support, (g) strong commitment, (h) sustaining the system, and (i) systematic ongoing professional development.

■ PRIMARY FOCUS

The schoolwide discipline plan is established to provide a positive school climate, and to create a supportive environment for personal, social, and academic growth for students and staff. In other words, the schoolwide plan is essentially an instrument to enable the goals of the school to be achieved, especially the goals of student achievement. Zins and Ponti (1990) concluded that it really does not matter how powerful a program may be, it probably will not succeed if the host environment does not support the process.

■ SYSTEMIC APPROACH

Strong emphasis is placed in this book on building systems. That is, the approach is not a strategy, a package, or a product. Rather, the approach is designed to address the needs of the whole school, which includes all students, all staff, and all settings. A crucial assumption in this model is that all features are necessary, and all features interact, functioning as a dynamic and organic system.

Systems theory was promulgated as early as the 1940s by a prominent biologist, Ludwig von Bertalanffy, who advocated that entities such as the human body cannot be properly understood by focusing on the properties of the parts. Rather, he argued that the focus needs to be on the "arrangement of and relations between the parts which connect them into the whole" (as cited in Heylighen & Joslyn, 1992, p. 1).

Schools also need to be viewed as an intricate system. Any innovation or program that is implemented must be carried out in a way that fully addresses the impact this program will have on the whole system. Additional detail is provided in Chapter 11, which describes systemic strategies that ensure the plan is sustained.

INSTRUCTIONAL APPROACH

Historically, school discipline has been operationalized in terms of rules and consequences. That is, if a rule was broken, negative consequences were delivered. This model is best described as a punitive or reactive approach. In contrast, the procedures outlined in this manual take a proactive approach. A strong emphasis is placed on staff taking concrete steps to systematically teach expected behaviors and use strategies to encourage and maintain these behaviors once learned. The focus is on establishing and maintaining the specific student behaviors that help students to become successful in school. In addition, the fundamental strategy for establishing these schoolwide behavior expectations is to adapt instructional practices used to teach academic skills. Proactive, in this sense, is understood to mean the teaching of behavior.

CONTINUUM OF POSITIVE BEHAVIOR AND ACADEMIC SUPPORT

The schoolwide discipline plan represents a first and necessary step in a continuum for providing behavior support to all students. In general, the student body can be divided into three groups (see Figure 2.1: Distribution of Student Population).

The first group, the base of the triangle, represents approximately 80% of the student population. These students, by and large, are relatively successful at school and respond positively to a proactive schoolwide discipline plan. The second group, comprising 10% to 15% of students, is classified as at risk. These students can become successful in school with more specialized support beyond the schoolwide plan. The final group, representing approximately 5% of the student body, is classified as special-needs students or students in crisis. These students need individualized and usually intensive support services.

It is important to note that the schoolwide plan is usually insufficient to meet the needs of the at-risk and special-needs students. In effect, the schoolwide plan is basically designed for the first group of students (the 80% group). However, once the proactive schoolwide plan is in place, school personnel are freer to address the needs of the more-involved students. Moreover, if the interventions used for the at-risk and special-needs groups become successful, an effective schoolwide plan will provide the supportive environment needed to maintain these changes.

Figure 2.1   Distribution of Student Population

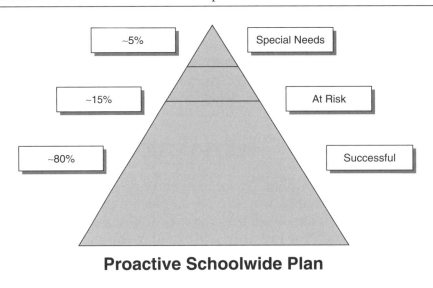

Proactive Schoolwide Plan

SOURCE: Adapted with permission from the OSEP Center on Positive and Behavioral Interventions and Supports (2004).

■ A BUILDING LEADERSHIP TEAM-BASED APPROACH

The schoolwide discipline plan presented in this book is founded on a team-based process. This means that very careful attention is given in the initial planning to ensure that all stakeholders know their roles and responsibilities and that a systematic structure is in place to ensure that adequate and timely information is communicated on details for all phases of implementation and maintenance.

With due deliberation, a team is selected that is representative of the major groups in the school. This team includes teachers from the various grade levels, administration personnel, and certified and classified staff. This team provides the necessary leadership for the development, implementation, and maintenance of the plan.

Researchers have found that effective operation of a team-based process is the key to successful implementation of a schoolwide plan (Colvin et al., 1993; OSEP Center on Positive and Behavioral Interventions and Supports, 2004; Sprick, Sprick, & Garrison, 1992; Todd, Horner, Sugai, & Sprague, 1999). Roles for the staff and team are clearly defined. Careful guidelines are developed to ensure all staff members have an opportunity to provide input in the development of the plan and to evaluate and revise the plan as needed.

■ STRONG COMMITMENT

For staff to undertake developing and implementing a proactive school-wide discipline plan, there needs to be strong agreement among staff that this activity will be one of the major priorities for the school year. Considerable time and effort needs to be given to the undertaking. If the plan is not a priority, it will more than likely fail. Once the school makes such an activity a major priority, the district needs to be in tune with the requirements and demands of such an endeavor and provide appropriate support. The school and district need to make a long-term or ongoing commitment to this initiative.

DATA-BASED DECISION-MAKING PROCESS ■

A data management system is absolutely essential for the development and maintenance of a proactive schoolwide plan. Data collected are used to monitor progress, make decisions, and provide a basis for evaluating these decisions. Data are also used for dissemination to faculty, district office representatives, board members, and stakeholders as appropriate. Developing an effective and efficient data management system and using this information in productive ways is a major key for a proactive discipline plan.

SUSTAINING THE SYSTEM ■

There is a common misconception in school improvement plans that once the plan has been developed and effectively implemented, it will sustain itself. The literature on school reform reports the opposite. Plans do not sustain themselves; they simply begin to be dropped and fail. Systematic planning needs to be in place for a system to be sustained. Specifically, a team will always be needed (the composition of the team may and will change). Administrative and district support will also be needed. One reason is that there are continual changes in student population and turnover within the faculty. In addition, other pressures or challenges may be imposed on the school or district, making it necessary to have a strong, positive school climate to meet these changes.

SYSTEMATIC ONGOING ■
PROFESSIONAL DEVELOPMENT

Provision for ongoing professional development is a key feature for planning, developing, implementing, and sustaining a proactive schoolwide discipline plan. There are always new staff members coming on board, and some staff may need more training than others. Moreover, some staff may begin to drop some of the initial practices that ensured success early in implementation. The key to professional development for a schoolwide effort is that all staff must be involved. So-called one-shot workshops attended by a few faculty usually will not lead to successful schoolwide endeavors. All staff must be targeted and involved. There needs to be a planned agenda, often spanning several years, to cover the range of content needed for successful implementation.

■ SUMMARY

The key underpinning of this book is that a proactive approach to school discipline is used in the design of the plan. The assumption is that the faculty focus on establishing the desirable behaviors necessary for the proper functioning of the school. Specifically, these behaviors are identified and then systematically and explicitly taught. A team-based process is used to implement the plan. This team, representative of the whole faculty, provides the leadership to ensure the various components of the plan are developed, implemented, and maintained.

3

Vital Role of the Principal and Administrative Support

Much has been written over the past two decades on the very broad subject of school reform. One irrefutable finding is the importance of the role of the school administration, and in particular, the leadership role of the principal. Several writers and researchers have concluded that when a principal is not solidly behind school improvement plans, the process is likely to stumble and dissipate (Colvin, Kame'enui, & Sugai, 1993; Frase, 2005; Fullan, 2002; Sprick, Wise, Marcum, Haykim, & Howard, 2005; Sugai, 1996). Some staff may expend considerable energy initially but lose heart when the principal does not support the process at critical steps. These staff members, who are often building leaders, usually become reluctant to undertake leadership roles in the future.

Several examples of the importance and effectiveness of the principal's leadership role will be described, followed by specific information on how a principal may provide administrative support for school innovations.

EXEMPLARS OF EFFECTIVE ADMINISTRATIVE SUPPORT ■

In 1997, an important alliance was formed consisting of a permanent partnership of leading educational organizations in America called the

"Learning First Alliance" (Togneri & Anderson, 2003). This alliance was charged with a twofold mission to (a) locate low-income school districts that had significantly raised student achievement, and (b) identify the common key variables within these that contributed to their success.

The alliance found only isolated islands of excellence and reported that five high-poverty school districts had significantly raised student achievement. For example, in one successful district in 1994, 65% of African American students met minimum expectations compared with 84% of white students. By 2002, the percentage of students meeting minimum requirements had risen to 94% for African American and to 96% for white students (Togneri & Anderson, 2003). Both groups clearly improved.

The next step involved conducting extensive surveys in each of these effective school districts to identify the factors that contributed to their impressive gains in student learning. The results were alarmingly simple. Two factors emerged that were consistently identified by each district in this order: (a) Each district developed a supportive infrastructure at district level with clearly delineated and integrated roles for the entire school administration, including the school board, superintendents, and principals, and (b) each district addressed and implemented instructional practices that have a solid research base in terms of implementation and effectiveness.

In summary, the role of administrative support was clearly a predominant factor in enabling these five school districts to show substantial improvement in student learning. The reader is referred to the Web site www.learningfirst.org, for full access to this report.

In a similar endeavor, the Wallace Foundation in 2004 sponsored a project to conduct an extensive review of research literature to determine the role of administrative leadership in student learning, in particular in relation to gains in academic achievement. The report concluded, "The total (direct and indirect) effects of leadership on student learning account for about a quarter of the total school effects" (Leithwood, Seashore Louis, Anderson, & Wahlstrom, 2004, p. 5). In effect, leadership was identified as second only to classroom instruction among all school-related factors that contribute to what students learn at school.

Several authors have reported the critical role that principals play in creating the kind of school environment necessary for school reform or for school improvement plans to be effectively implemented. For example, Fullan (2002) noted, "School improvement will depend on principals who can foster the conditions necessary for sustained educational reform in a complex rapidly changing society" (p. 16). In addition, Hargreaves and Fink (2006), in a thorough review of research on sustaining school reform, concluded, "Sustainable improvement depends on successful leadership" (p. 1).

It appears indisputable that the building principal is the key to any major schoolwide staff development activity. Consequently, any school improvement or reform effort needs to have solid and clearly defined support from the principal for the endeavor to succeed.

ADMINISTRATIVE SUPPORT IN IMPLEMENTING ◼ A SCHOOLWIDE DISCIPLINE PLAN

While the concept of administrative support is deemed necessary for effective school improvement, it is somewhat elusive to define. One way to clarify the concept is to ask, "What does a principal actually do to provide administrative support?" or "What does administrative support really look like?" One principal may provide administrative support intuitively and have teachers who are well aware and appreciative of that support. Another principal may attempt to provide administrative support, yet teachers view the support as inconsistent or even manipulative. Still a third principal may say, "Tell me what administrative support is and I will do it. Presently, I do not know exactly what it is." In this section, we present a detailed analysis of administrative support by examining the role of the principal in the development and implementation of a comprehensive and proactive schoolwide discipline plan. The major concepts are adapted with permission from a published article by Colvin and Sprick (1999). While leadership styles may vary, the following 13 strategies have been identified as critical activities that a principal needs to engage in to provide administrative support to effect change in a school (Box 3.1).

These strategies concretely define how a principal can provide administrative support for school-reform efforts and are derived from working in public schools with a large number of principals, reviewing research and best practices in administrative leadership, and implementing programs and plans in more than 70 elementary and secondary schools. Each

---

BOX 3.1   Thirteen Strategies That Principals Need to Effect Change

1. Maintain standards

2. Make a public statement of support

3. Establish a leadership team

4. Support the team members

5. Guide the decision-making process

6. Take a leadership role in problem solving

7. Support the team meetings

8. Provide recognition to the faculty and team for their work

9. Serve as the point person for school-related groups

10. Monitor implementation activities and provide feedback

11. Review data and provide feedback regularly

12. Ensure innovation is sustained

13. Make a time commitment

SOURCE: Adapted from Colvin and Sprick (1999).

support strategy is described and illustrated in terms of the principal's role in working with staff to develop and implement a proactive school-wide discipline plan.

1. Maintain Standards

Perhaps the most important role an administrator has in supporting staff development and change in a school is to maintain standards, that is, to serve as a "gatekeeper." Many ideas and activities are presented to schools under the umbrella of professional development and school reform. However, all innovations are not equal. In fact, some can be quite destructive. A school administrator needs to carefully lead staff toward innovations that have a high probability of creating a positive effect (based on research or best practices) for the students and to lead staff away from innovations that will be ineffective or destructive. In this way, the principal serves as a gatekeeper for establishing, administering, and maintaining standards. However, these standards should not be arbitrary. They should be *policy* (Carnine, 1997). The role then becomes one of implementing and maintaining this policy.

2. Make a Public Statement of Support

Once a faculty has made a decision to implement a given innovation, the principal should follow with a public statement of support for the project—essentially, to inform the staff that whatever is possible and reasonable will be done to work with them in accomplishing the goals of the project (Box 3.2). However, if the principal does not follow through, credibility with staff will be eroded. Conversely, when follow-through occurs, credibility is enhanced, making it easier to undertake subsequent desirable projects.

3. Establish a Leadership Team

A critical task for a principal is to establish a building team to lead the process (Box 3.3). Since staff will be the people who must carry out most

---

BOX 3.2   Illustration of a Principal's Public Statement of Support

The staff and parent representatives at Jackson Middle School determine that developing a more comprehensive schoolwide discipline policy would move the school in the direction of their school vision. Therefore, the principal, Dr. Lee, publicly announces the goal of the school improvement effort during a faculty meeting, at a parent meeting, and in the staff bulletin and school newsletter. In each of these announcements, she stresses that she will actively support this effort to develop a more comprehensive discipline policy. She clearly articulates that the intent of the project is to develop and potentially revise procedures for managing behavior and motivating students and that the goals include reducing misbehavior, increasing student motivation, ensuring adequate and safe supervision, and improving school climate.

SOURCE: Colvin and Sprick (1999).

of the work, a successful innovation must have the support of staff. Successful development and implementation are more likely if staff play an active role in the process from the beginning. Therefore, the team needs to be representative of all the people who will be directly affected by the innovation. Using a team will save time because the entire faculty is relieved of the burden of participating in all aspects of planning. In addition, procedures need to be identified for determining the size of the team, usually five to seven members, and a process developed for selecting team members.

BOX 3.3   Illustration of a Principal's Role in Forming a Leadership Team

Example: Dr. Lee proposes to staff that a team consisting of the following seven positions be formed:

- Teacher representative for the sixth grade
- Teacher representative for the seventh grade
- Teacher representative for the eighth grade
- Representative for counselors and specialists
- Representative for paraprofessionals and secretaries
- Representative for the parent advisory committees
- Representative for administrative staff

She suggests that the time commitment for committee members will be a one-hour meeting after school every other Wednesday and suggests that each of the identified groups assume responsibility for selecting their own representative. After discussing this proposal, staff agrees with the team composition proposed by Dr. Lee and agrees to select their representatives by the first committee meeting, which has been set for two weeks hence.

SOURCE: Colvin and Sprick (1999).

---

4. Support the Team Members

Team members who participate in schoolwide projects and activities make a substantial commitment to the school. The principal can acknowledge their commitment by making a special visit to each team member, thanking them for agreeing to serve on the team, and assuring them that they will be provided help whenever possible. Another way to support team members is to be sensitive to their workload. For example, the principal might ensure that members of the team are not expected to serve on other committees. In other words, these team members should not be over-taxed. When the team needs significant amounts of time for certain tasks, the principal can offer assistance such as secretarial time or use substitute teachers to free team members. The principal can take steps to ensure that the team and faculty have consistent opportunities to develop and implement the schoolwide plan (Box 3.4). For example, it is important not to schedule other meetings involving team members at the times the team regularly meets. Also, it is important to allocate and maintain time for the project or activity at faculty meetings and to avoid taking this time away on the basis that "we have a full agenda." In addition, the principal can preserve the meeting space for the team and not "bump" the team to some other place because of a "more important" meeting.

BOX 3.4   Illustration of a Principal's Role in Supporting Team Members

As each group selects its representative for the team, Dr. Lee pays a short visit to the selected representatives. She thanks each person for his or her commitment and briefly reviews the long-term goals of the project. She also lets the representatives know that she is confident that they will not only represent their particular groups in the process, but that as individuals, each will bring a unique and valuable perspective to the committee meetings.

During the first meeting, Dr. Lee and Mr. Tomason (the assistant principal) inform the group that four times during the year, substitutes will be hired to cover their responsibilities so that they can have four full planning days—in addition to the every other Wednesday meetings. Also, Mr. Tomason will coordinate secretarial staff to assist the team with any clerical tasks (e.g., typing and printing) that need to be accomplished.

SOURCE: Colvin and Sprick (1999).

5. Guide the Decision-Making Processes

Effective administrators are very clear about the school's process for decision making in relation to school improvement issues. They inform staff in advance regarding the nature of any decisions that must be made about particular issues, and they have in place clear and agreed-on processes for staff to reach a decision. One such process is a simple vote, either majority rules or something like 70% majority if a greater level of commitment on the part of faculty is needed. The disadvantage of a simple vote is that it is possible that some percentage of the faculty, those people who must carry out any decisions that are made, may actively object to the outcome of the decision.

An alternative to the simple vote, one that may facilitate greater commitment on the part of all staff, is a procedure called "fist of five." In this method, each faculty member votes by holding up one to five fingers. Holding up five fingers means, "I actively support this decision and will even take a leadership role in carrying out the decision." Four fingers means, "I actively support this decision, but choose not to take a leadership role." Three fingers means, "I support this decision." Two fingers means, "I have reservations about this decision, but I will not roadblock implementation." One finger means, "I have strong objections and cannot support, and will even roadblock this decision." Under the fist of five procedure, if anyone votes a "one finger," the decision will not be made at that moment. However, the people voting "one finger" are responsible for voicing their concerns. This gives staff in favor of the decision an opportunity to modify the plan in a way that those opposing can accept. This method of decision making reduces the passive resistance to a decision that a simple majority vote can sometimes create (Box 3.5).

6. Take a Leadership Role in Problem Solving

If problems arise within the team and resolution does not occur, the principal needs to be ready to address the problems and find solutions in a timely manner. Similarly, if problems occur between the team and faculty or within faculty over some aspect of the plan, the principal has

---

BOX 3.5   Illustration of a Principal Guiding Decision Making

The committee responsible for carrying out the decision to design and implement a new schoolwide discipline plan proposes to the total staff that use of administrative involvement in discipline (i.e., sending students to the office) be limited to illegal acts, physically dangerous acts, and the overt and immediate refusal to comply. After discussing the issue, a "fist of five" vote is taken. Three staff members vote "one," and the rest of the votes are "three" or higher. Dr. Lee declares that there was no additional time in the meeting that day, but the committee needed to contact the three people who voted "one finger" to learn about these individuals' objections to the proposed policy.

During the next week, the committee members discuss the issue privately with the three teachers. Their concern was that although the three criteria proposed made sense, they know that sometimes there is a student who might exhibit less severe behavior, but does it so chronically and frequently that administrative involvement might be warranted. The committee's concern is that some teachers might overuse referral for every minor behavior. In fact, that is the current situation the policy is supposed to reduce. After some discussion and negotiation, the committee and the three teachers add a fourth criterion to the list. In addition to the three mentioned previously, teachers could send a student to the office for less severe infractions (e.g., frequent disruptive behavior) if the matter is discussed in advance with either the principal or the assistant principal, and they agree that the next time the behavior occurs, the student can be sent to the office.

At the next faculty meeting, the four criteria were proposed. Every faculty member voted four or higher. Dr. Lee publicly thanks the committee and thanks the people who had previously voted one. She informs the entire staff that the initial objections and the skill of the committee and the people who voted one have resulted in a policy that was much better than the original plan.

SOURCE: Colvin and Sprick (1999).

---

a clear role in assisting with the problem solving. This does not mean "taking over." Rather, it involves stepping in and leading the group to a workable solution. For example, some team members may find it difficult to work effectively with certain staff members due to personality issues or a past history of conflict. In these cases, the administrator might visit with involved staff, remind them of the long-term vision of the school, and encourage staff to cooperate for the "good of the order."

Principals should avoid rhetoric, especially in the context of problem solving. Typically, teachers are not impressed with administrative jargon. They need plain talk that is sincere and clear (Box 3.6).

7. Support the Team Meetings

If the principal is a member of the team, then it is important to attend meetings (Box 3.7). Missing a meeting should be the exception. If the principal is frequently absent (as a team member), a wrong message is sent to the team, that is, "It is important for you to be there, but not me." In cases in which the vice-principal is the administrative representative, the principal should still attend meetings on an intermittent basis to demonstrate support. Note that the principal should use the opportunity to thank staff for their time and effort on a regular basis.

BOX 3.6　Illustration of a Principal Taking a Leadership Role in Problem Solving

As part of their plan for improving hallway behavior, the staff of Jackson Middle School agree that students who must go from one place to another during class time will be required to have a hall pass. In addition, staff agree that during passing periods, staff members should be out in the halls monitoring student behavior, correcting misbehavior, and interacting in a friendly manner with students engaged in appropriate behavior. During the initial discussion of these issues, three teachers express the belief that they should not have to "police the halls." These staff members state that since they manage student behavior in the classroom, they should not have to be responsible for the students' hallway behavior. However, they agree to go along with the decision.

Once the new procedures have been implemented, it becomes apparent that these staff members are not following through on supervising hallway behavior. The other teachers in their wing begin feeling overburdened and resentful about having to do all of the hallway monitoring. As tensions increase, Dr. Lee intervenes by meeting individually with each of these three staff members. Her approach is to communicate to staff that there is a problem and that a solution needs to be found. She discusses the need for the monitoring and explores other options. She also explores the difficulties with remembering to monitor the hallways and examines some strategies for providing reminders. Each teacher, while not exactly pleased with the monitoring plan, agrees to implement the plan. Dr. Lee assures each teacher that the plan will be reviewed toward the end of the term and that other options will be considered at that time if problems persist.

SOURCE: Colvin and Sprick (1999).

BOX 3.7　Illustration of a Principal Supporting Team Meetings

As the administration's representative, Mr. Tomason, the assistant principal, attends every meeting. Dr. Lee makes periodic visits to the meetings. However, Dr. Lee has made it clear that if there is an issue that warrants the principal's input, she is to be directly invited to the meeting and apprised of the issue. She announces that she will attend the next meeting to discuss the issue.

SOURCE: Colvin and Sprick (1999).

---

8. Provide Recognition to the Faculty and Team for Their Work

The administrator has a major role in showing appreciation to the team and faculty for their efforts. Whenever major projects or activities are undertaken, the principal should take steps to acknowledge involved staff (such as visits with the staff individually and use of staff notices, staff bulletins, and staff meetings to acknowledge the work and effort by team members; Box 3.8).

9. Serve as the Point Person for School-Related Groups

Another important role for the principal is to provide ongoing information about the project's goals and activities to key school groups such as the site-based council, the student council, district organizations, and parent organizations (Box 3.9). Team members could be involved in these

---

BOX 3.8   Illustration of a Principal Recognizing Team Members

Dr. Lee checks to see when each of the team members has his or her prep period for the day. She then visits them during this time to personally thank them for their willingness to serve on the team. She acknowledges their role and effort and assures them that she and the staff are grateful to them. Dr. Lee also lists the team on the front page of the staff newsletter and expresses her thanks to the team. At a faculty meeting, she reads a list of the team members and asks faculty to show their appreciation by giving them a round of applause.

SOURCE: Colvin and Sprick (1999).

BOX 3.9   Illustration of a Principal Serving as Point Person

At one point, the parent representative gives a report on the team's goals and progress to the Parent-Teacher Association meeting. She mentions that one of the goals of the group is to get the faculty to spend more time at the beginning of the next school year teaching students social skills, specifically how to behave responsibly in common areas such as the cafeteria and halls. No one at the meeting expresses any concerns or problems.

Three days later, a scathing letter appears on the editorial page of the local paper. A parent has written that the school is planning to stop teaching academics and spend all the time "teaching social skills and having students contemplating their navels."

Dr. Lee arranges to meet directly with this particular parent and any others who share her concern. At this meeting, Dr. Lee assures the parents that any social skills instruction will be done for the purpose of enhancing learning of academics. Although some parents are still concerned, no more letters appear. Dr. Lee stays in direct contact with the person who wrote the letter to keep her informed and to alleviate her concerns.

SOURCE: Colvin and Sprick (1999).

---

presentations as appropriate as a way of giving them some recognition. It is important to acknowledge the work of the team and staff and address problems in a timely manner if they arise.

10. Monitor Implementation Activities and Provide Feedback

The principal has a vital role in observing and monitoring the actual implementation of the school project, particularly activities that the faculty has decided to undertake. Staff need to see tangible evidence of the principal's interest in and concern for the particular activity being implemented. In other words, the principal needs to be visible "when the rubber hits the road." The principal should provide specific praise and recognition to staff members implementing the new procedures. In this way, support and an example are provided to staff regarding the activity under implementation. Moreover, the principal is in a good position to assess progress. Observations can be discussed with the team or the entire faculty.

Another common problem during the implementation of any innovation is that some staff will not follow through on the new procedures. Possible actions by the principal include visiting with these staff members, providing reminders during a faculty meeting regarding the agreed-on procedures, or turning the problem back to the team to develop proposed

---

> **BOX 3.10   Illustration of a Principal's Role in Monitoring Implementation**
>
> Dr. Lee makes a concerted effort to be out in the halls during passing periods and before and after school. In this way, she models for staff how to interact in a friendly way with students and how to correct misbehavior when necessary. This also lets staff who are in the hall know that Dr. Lee is aware they are meeting the agreed-on commitment. Finally, her visibility in the hallway serves as a reminder to staff who may not be following through with the plan.
>
> Once the hallway behavior improves significantly, the team decides to address developing schoolwide policies and procedures to increase the rate of homework completion. Dr. Lee responds that this is an excellent next step and publicly expresses her support.
>
> SOURCE: Colvin and Sprick (1999).

---

solutions. Regardless of how the problem is addressed, the principal must follow through to see that all staff are now implementing the agreed-on procedures. Staff need to know that their cooperation is expected, implementation will be monitored, and, if there is a problem, efforts will be made to find a solution (Box 3.10).

11. Review Data and Provide Feedback Regularly

The procedures for collecting data to monitor progress and for use in decision making will be described in detail in Chapter 10. In this section, it is essential for the principal to take an active interest in data collection and discussions regarding the results. The ideal situation regarding data collection is to appoint someone on the team to manage the data collection and to generate data summaries (Togneri & Anderson, 2003). In this way, the principal is one of the recipients of the regular data summaries.

12. Ensure Innovation Is Sustained

A very common trap for schools to fall into following a successful innovation is to slowly allow the procedures to disappear. One reason is that the initial overt problems have been addressed successfully. For example, in the case of school discipline, initially there may have been an unacceptable number of fights between students or an inordinately high number of office referrals. Once the proactive schoolwide plan has been implemented, significant reductions occur in the number of student fights or office referrals. As a result, the faculty may be less vigilant or concerned about following the procedures. Another reason for program drift is that another innovation is imposed on staff or staff may initiate another innovation. The result is that this new innovation takes everyone's time and energy so that the prior program is systematically dropped. The principal must play a critical role in setting expectations that time, effort, and support are not only necessary to develop and implement the schoolwide plan, but resources must be allocated to sustain the plan over time. Moreover, the principal communicates that each year, there are new staff and new students so the procedural steps for implementing the plan need to be maintained each year (Box 3.11).

> **Box 3.11   Illustration of a Principal Ensuring Sustainability of a Plan**
>
> When the faculty at Jackson Middle School decide that they want to develop and implement a proactive schoolwide discipline plan, Dr. Lee reminds them that this endeavor cannot be a one- or two-year endeavor. A plan such as this needs to be not only developed and implemented but also needs to be sustained for years to come.
>
> Moreover, two years later, the faculty has noted the data on the schoolwide discipline plan have been very successful—office referrals are down, problems in common settings of hallways and the cafeteria are quite minimal, and more and more students are receiving the good citizen awards. At this point, the faculty wants to address reading and literacy on a schoolwide basis. Dr. Lee immediately acknowledges the wonderful improvement in behavior schoolwide and affirms the need to address literacy. However, she cautions that the schoolwide discipline procedures must still be followed and maintained. The new focus of literacy must be implemented in conjunction with the schoolwide discipline plan. In other words, we cannot drop one successful program to address another need. Rather, we address the new need and at the same time find ways to sustain the previous innovation, schoolwide discipline.
>
> SOURCE: Colvin and Sprick (1999).

13. Make a Time Commitment

Finally, principals must realize that the process for effective change takes time. While there is often an urgency to bring about substantial changes, researchers have pointed out for many years that it takes time for faculty to make the necessary commitments and adjustments to bring about these changes (Fullan, 2003; Gersten & Woodward, 1990; Guskey, 1986; Hord, Rutherford, Huling, & Hall, 2004; Smylie, 1988). Given that a schoolwide proactive discipline plan must involve all faculty, all settings, and all students, Colvin et al. (1993) found in Project PREPARE that it was only in the second year that it could be said the plan was firmly in place.

In effect, while principals have to be responsive to their school needs, there has to be an element of caution, as it takes time to bring all people on board and to implement the plan consistently. The best suggestion is for the principal to be quietly persistent in bringing the faculty along and have the understanding that in general, it takes time, generally a year or two, for effective and durable change to occur.

SUMMARY ■

There is general consensus among educators that schools are under tremendous pressure to address a wide and expanding range of social problems. These demands often translate to school improvement efforts. Research has identified administrative support as a critical component needed for school improvement and successful staff development activities. Although administrative support is a widely held value in schools, it is elusive to define. In this chapter, 13 practical strategies that principals can implement have been described and illustrated to effectively operationalize administrative support. If principals use these strategies, staff development will be more successful, and the faculty and students will be more likely to achieve their goals.

4

Establishing a Building Leadership Team

At the heart of the system process recommended in this book is the proper functioning of a building leadership team. This team, composed of representatives of the school administration, faculty, and staff, serves as a catalyst for the process and provides ongoing leadership to ensure the various steps in the process and details of the plan are implemented with fidelity. The following eight steps in the process are now described: (a) establishing the need for a plan, (b) conducting a schoolwide discipline plan survey, (c) securing initial commitments, (d) forming a building leadership team, (e) establishing roles and responsibilities, (f) developing a communication system, (g) developing an ongoing decision-making process, and (h) following a checklist for building leadership team-based process.

ESTABLISHING THE NEED FOR A PLAN ■

The need for developing a schoolwide discipline plan can arise through a number of factors, such as unacceptable rates of office referrals for discipline issues; a number of serious incidences that impact school safety; ongoing complaints from parents and community members; the school or district getting a bad reputation for poor academic performance and problem behavior; high rates of staff turnover, resignations, and requests for transfers; and word-of-mouth reports from educators or parents familiar with the positive results obtained in other schools through adopting a plan.

It is very important to discuss this new schoolwide discipline plan in the light of existing school improvement plans. Ideally, the schoolwide plan may provide some impetus or clarity to the current school improvement plans. It is also important to integrate this plan with existing plans as far as possible. If some level of integration and accommodations are not made in the initial planning, there is the risk of overloading or confusing staff.

■ CONDUCTING A SCHOOLWIDE DISCIPLINE PLAN SURVEY

If there is any sense that a plan may be needed in a school, it is highly recommended to have all faculty members complete the following survey: Appendix A: Form 4.1, Checklist for Determining the Adequacy of an Existing Schoolwide Discipline Plan. This simple survey is designed to assess the extent to which the essential components of a schoolwide plan are already in place (these components are fully described in Section II, Chapters 5–11). There is no assumption that every school needs to abandon what it has in place already and adopt the plan described in this book. Rather, the assumption is to identify and use the components of the existing plan that are in place and working, to identify where the gaps are, and then to develop a comprehensive plan based on these findings.

This survey can also serve as a pre-post measure. The survey is completed and scored before the proactive schoolwide plan is implemented to obtain a starting point measure. The survey is then completed in subsequent years to measure the changes that may have occurred following implementation.

The scoring is meant to be very simple. The score "yes" means that the item is firmly in place to a reasonable extent. The score "no" means that the item is not in place and needs attention to have it more fully in place.

The decision rules are based on scores from a relatively large number of schools around the nation that have implemented a proactive schoolwide discipline plan. The criterion of an average score of less than 8 out of 12 means that there is a need to fully implement a schoolwide plan. An average score of 8 or more out of 12 means that a lot of the components of a schoolwide plan are in place and pinpoints can be made to target the specific areas that need attention.

■ SECURING INITIAL COMMITMENTS

Once there is some consensus that the school or district would benefit from adopting a positive schoolwide plan, there needs to be a clear-cut process for obtaining a firm commitment from all involved parties. First and foremost, the school administration, faculty, and staff must make a firm commitment to make this activity a major priority. In addition, there should be a formal procedure by which the entire faculty votes on whether they want to commit to adopting a plan. In some cases, because of urgency arising from behavior issues, schools are mandated to develop a plan to improve their situation. In these cases, there needs to be clear communication to all faculty and staff of the urgency of the situation and of the need to adopt a plan.

Appendix A

Form 4.1   Checklist for Determining the Adequacy of an Existing Schoolwide Discipline Plan

YES NO	1.	The purpose of schoolwide discipline is clearly stated.
YES NO	2.	Schoolwide behavior expectations are clearly stated.
YES NO	3.	Schoolwide procedures are in place to teach expected behaviors.
YES NO	4.	Schoolwide practices are in place to recognize demonstrations of expected behavior.
YES NO	5.	Staff members are clear as to which behavior should be dealt with by staff and which should warrant office referrals.
YES NO	6.	Procedures are in place for staff to work together to address persistent, minor behavior.
YES NO	7.	A continuum of steps is available to address serious office-referral–level behavior.
YES NO	8.	Procedures are in place to use building resources to assist students who display chronic, serious behavior.
YES NO	9.	Procedures are in place to address crises or emergencies.
YES NO	10.	Data-keeping procedures are in place to track student behavior.
YES NO	11.	Data are used to make planning decisions.
YES NO	12.	Procedures are in place to sustain the plan.

_____   Number of YES items

_____   Number of NO items

MARK DECISION

_____ *More than eight YES responses:* Maintain existing program and develop plan to address inadequacies, if necessary.

_____ *Fewer than eight YES responses:* Establish and develop a building leadership team to assist staff in developing a proactive schoolwide discipline plan.

In addition to securing a commitment from the school, commitment must also be assured from the district office, including key administrators such as the superintendent and supervisors. The school board should be apprised of the needs basis for adopting a plan and commit its support as well.

Part of the commitment, especially from the administration, is to ensure that the school or district can allocate the resources, both short and long term, and rearrange resources as needed. For example, professional development may be needed to train all staff in the procedures, consultants initially may be necessary, the leadership team may need release time to set up the procedures on a periodic basis, and there may be costs associated with obtaining materials.

Finally, the members of the leadership team must commit to attending the meetings, undertaking resulting tasks, and providing ongoing leadership as needed.

■ FORMING A BUILDING LEADERSHIP TEAM

The leadership for the schoolwide plan is provided by a building team. The most important point here is that the team should be truly representative of the naturally occurring groups in the school including administrators, grade-level teachers, support personnel such as school psychologists and counselors, classified staff, general-education and special-education teachers (weighted toward general-education teachers), and parents and students as appropriate.

The team representatives can be selected by (a) election, in which each group selects its own representative; (b) volunteers, in which staff members from each group volunteer their services; or (c) appointment, in which, for example, the administrator appoints representatives. While various combinations of these procedures for team selection may work, the election process is probably the best way to select members. The reason is that all staff can have input regarding the selection, and there is more likelihood of staff with the most credibility and leadership skills being selected. The administrator may need to step in and appoint someone, or more exactly, persuade someone to step in, if a key group has failed to produce a representative.

■ ESTABLISHING ROLES AND RESPONSIBILITIES

In developing a proactive schoolwide discipline plan, the whole school community has some level of involvement and responsibility. Clearly the principal or school administrator and building leadership team will have most of the responsibility for developing, implementing, and maintaining the plan. However, there is no sense that responsibility is solely theirs. The entire school community (school board members, the superintendent, the district office, administrators, faculties, staff, parents, students, and community members) has a role in supporting the plan, responding to the data reports, providing levels of accountability as appropriate, and providing ongoing feedback and input. It is crucial that the building leadership team take necessary steps early in the development of the plan to inform the various stakeholders of the importance of their roles and that progress information and results be disseminated on a regular basis for their review and response.

DEVELOPING A COMMUNICATION AND COORDINATION SYSTEM ◼

Once the system process has been established by which administrative support for all stakeholders has been obtained and the building leadership team has been formed, the next step is to develop a systematic communication and coordination system. There are five steps to this process: (a) forming a communication system for the team, (b) creating a team meeting structure, (c) coordinating team and faculty meetings, (d) following a decision-making process, and (e) following minute-taking procedures. Each of these steps is described with accompanying forms followed by a system-based checklist located in the Appendix section.

Communication System for the Building Leadership Team

It is standard practice in schools and school districts today to use e-mail as the major form of communication. The most common failure of this system is that some team members may not regularly check their e-mail or perhaps open the e-mail and not read the information. Printed notes, memos, and telephone messages are also commonly used. Team members must decide on a communication system and then commit to using the system. Appendix B: Form 4.2, Worksheet for a Leadership Team, provides a record of contact information for each member. This form should be completed at the team's first meeting.

Building Leadership Team Meeting Structure

The team needs to identify times and places for regular meetings. This information should be recorded (Appendix B: Form 4.2, Worksheet for a Leadership Team). It is recommended that the team meet at least every other week for 30 to 45 minutes. It is very critical for the meetings to start on time and end on time. Team members are busy people, and it can become frustrating for them if the meetings start late or finish late. The meetings need to be very focused, businesslike, and efficient. It is helpful for a team member to watch the clock and alert members if the meeting is dragging or if the pace is too slow to address all items on the agenda.

Coordination of Building Leadership Team and Faculty Meetings

It is absolutely necessary that the team meet with the faculty on a regular basis regarding the development and implementation of the discipline plan. This information is also recorded (Appendix B: Form 4.2, Worksheet for a Leadership Team). In some cases, a special faculty meeting can be

Appendix B

Form 4.2   Worksheet for a Leadership Team

Name of School _____

Name	Title	E-mail	Telephone (Extension or Cell)
Group E-mail			

Team Meetings

Frequency _____   Location _____

Time   _____   Day   _____

Faculty Meetings

Frequency _____   Location _____

Time   _____   Day   _____

Allocated Time _____

Next Meeting Date _____

Decision Process and Criterion

Procedure _____

Criterion _____

called, but in general, it is better to take a fixed amount of time, say 10 to 15 minutes of the regular faculty meetings. Several schools adopted the practice of having team meetings during the first and third weeks of the month and faculty meetings during the second and fourth weeks. In these cases, the team was a standard item on the agenda (the team had 10–15 minutes to raise some aspects of the discipline plan).

Minute-Taking Procedures

The team meeting minutes provide an ongoing record of the meetings, decisions, activities, and related events. It is very helpful to use a generic form that is simply filled in at the meeting, copied, and distributed immediately following the meeting. Such a procedure lessens the burden for the team member taking notes. Also, by having a generic agenda, there is more likelihood for team members to stay on task and complete the agenda. It is recommended that the various roles in a meeting be shared evenly, especially by the note taker and the chair. Typically, the note taker is a different person than the chairperson. The chairperson needs to be free enough to keep the meeting focused and moving. The form presented in Appendix C: Form 4.3, Building Team Minutes, can serve as a guide to get started. The team should adapt the form to suit the team's specific needs.

DEVELOPING AN ONGOING ■
DECISION-MAKING PROCESS

It is crucial to establish a decision-making process, otherwise the whole operation may flounder because closure cannot be reached on some aspects of the plan. Typically, the team may present a draft to faculty, and faculty respond to the draft through discussion. Then it is time to vote. A mechanism for voting is needed (described in Chapter 3). If the criterion is not met, the team takes the item back to the table and develops another draft. Sometimes it may be necessary to have a "working plan." The reason is that something needs to be in place. Revisions can occur down the road as needed. For example, staff may not have reached agreement on the office-referral form. However, in these cases, a form needs to be used while closure is being obtained on the new form. Typically, schools use the existing forms until the replacement ones have been finalized.

FOLLOWING A CHECKLIST FOR ■
LEADERSHIP TEAM-BASED PROCESS

It cannot be stressed too much that careful attention needs to be given to developing a workable process for getting started, implementing, and maintaining the schoolwide plan. Granted, the plan itself must be evidence based and show every indication that the school or district will benefit considerably from adopting the plan. However, it is the process that will ensure that the plan is implemented with ongoing fidelity and that the

(Text continued on page 37)

Appendix C

Form 4.3 Building Team Minutes

School _____   Date _____

Present_____   _____

_____   _____

_____   _____

_____   _____

Time _____ to _____   Location _____

Updates

New Discussion/Activities

Decisions

Items to Present to Faculty

Items:

Team Member(s) Presenting Items:

Other

Next Meeting:

Next Chair:

Appendix D

Form 4.4   Checklist for Building Leadership Team-Based Process

Process Factor	In Place	
1. Establishing the Need for a Plan		
1.1 Schoolwide discipline plan survey conducted and scored	Yes	No
1.2 Results discussed at school or building level	Yes	No
1.3 Overview of plan (components and evidence base) presented to faculty or faculties	Yes	No
1.4 Stakeholders informed of plan:		
• School board	Yes	No
• District office	Yes	No
• Building administrators	Yes	No
• Faculties (see Item 2 below)	Yes	No
• Parents	Yes	No
• Students	Yes	No
1.5 Plan is integrated with existing school improvement plans as appropriate	Yes	No
2. Securing Initial Commitment of Faculty		
2.1 Faculty informed of results of needs assessment	Yes	No
2.2 Faculty presented with an overview of proactive schoolwide plan including data from other schools	Yes	No
2.3 Faculty presented with information relating the needs assessment and the plan	Yes	No
2.4 Faculty given opportunity to discuss merits and issues related to plan adoption	Yes	No
2.5 Criterion set for adoption of plan	Yes	No
2.6 Faculty has formal vote on adopting plan	Yes	No
2.7 Preliminary steps reviewed	Yes	No
2.8 Start date determined	Yes	No
2.9 Support expressed by other stakeholders	Yes	No
• School board		
• Superintendent		
• District personnel as appropriate		
• Parent bodies as appropriate		
• Student body as appropriate		
3. Forming a Building Leadership Team		
3.1 Role and responsibilities identified	Yes	No
3.2 Representative groups within faculty identified	Yes	No
3.3 Team selection process determined	Yes	No

(Continued)

Form 4.4 (Continued)

Process Factor	In Place	
3.4 Team selected	Yes	No
3.5 Team is representative of faculty groups	Yes	No
3.6 Faculty notified of team composition	Yes	No
3.7 Student representatives selected	Yes	No
3.8 Parent representatives selected	Yes	No
4. Establishing Roles and Responsibilities		
4.1 Principal	Yes	No
4.2 Team	Yes	No
4.3 Faculty	Yes	No
4.4 School board	Yes	No
4.5 Superintendent	Yes	No
4.6 District office	Yes	No
4.7 Parent body	Yes	No
4.8 Student	Yes	No
5. Developing a Communication System		
5.1 Team meeting scheduled (times and places)	Yes	No
5.2 Team note-taking process and within-team dissemination process determined	Yes	No
5.3 Process for team connecting with faculty determined	Yes	No
5.4 Dissemination process determined for outcomes to be shared with stakeholders	Yes	No
5.5 Structures developed to enable input from faculty and stakeholders	Yes	No
6. Developing an Ongoing Decision-Making Process		
6.1 Data review system developed for team	Yes	No
6.2 Data review system for faculty developed	Yes	No
6.3 Decision-making process developed for team	Yes	No
6.4 Decision-making process developed for faculty	Yes	No

(Text continued from page 33)

support structures necessary for implementation and maintenance are in place. To this end, Form 4.4 has been designed to enable a school or district to examine the extent to which the critical process steps have been followed. It is strongly suggested that an action plan be developed immediately for any items on the checklist that have not been implemented satisfactorily. In other words, the process steps need to be firmly in place before the plan is implemented. An administrator, in conjunction with a lead teacher, should have a completed copy of Appendix D: Form 4.4, Checklist for Building Leadership Team-Based Process.

SUMMARY ■

In this chapter, the various steps involved in developing a process for implementing a proactive schoolwide discipline plan with a building leadership team were described. The importance of establishing a workable process before any steps are made to address schoolwide behavior cannot be overstated. If a solid process is in place beforehand, then there is much more likelihood of success in implementing the plan. There are many stakeholders in school operations within the school, the district, and the community. Each of these stakeholders needs to know his or her roles and responsibilities so that everyone is on the same page with the plan. The converse is equally true. That is, if all of the stakeholders are not working together with the system, then the plan will fail or show minimal results. In this regard, it is particularly important that each step identified in the process checklist form is completed. In this way, a workable process can be established and the chance of a successful implementation and maintenance of the plan is significantly enhanced.

Section II

Components of a Proactive Schoolwide Discipline Plan

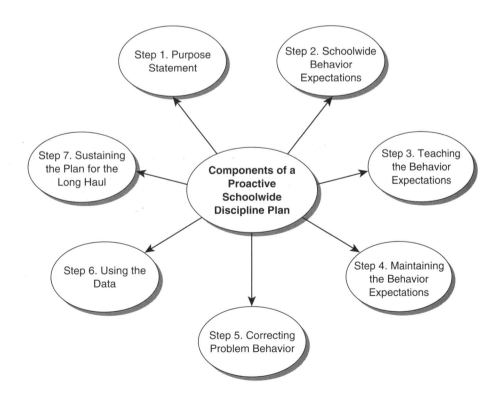

Public schools vary considerably in many domains, such as size, funding levels, age groups served, demographics, cultural factors, socioeconomic factors, and percentage of ethnically and culturally diverse students. The school discipline plan needs to be sensitive to these factors. In this section, while we describe the specific content components of a proactive schoolwide discipline plan, we strongly encourage each school or district to adapt the suggested procedures within these components to meet its unique needs.

The components of the proactive schoolwide discipline plan described in this section have been derived from initial research in Project PREPARE (Sugai, Kame'enui, & Colvin, 1990), from more than a decade of research and implementation by the Center on Positive and Behavioral Interventions and Supports (www.pbis.org), and from best practice procedures used by several school districts throughout America in implementing a schoolwide plan (Bear, 1990; Lewis & Sugai, 1999; Luiselli, Putnam, & Sunderland, 2002; Nelson, Martella, & Galand, 1998; Todd, Horner, Sugai, & Sprague, 1999).

There are seven components in this model that comprise the critical steps in developing a proactive schoolwide discipline plan: (a) creating a purpose statement, (b) establishing schoolwide behavior expectations, (c) teaching the behavior expectations, (d) maintaining the behavior expectations, (e) correcting problem behavior, (f) using the data, and (g) sustaining the plan for the long haul. These components are depicted in the figure on page 39. Each component will include a description and rationale, examples, checklists, and forms.

5

Step 1. Purpose Statement

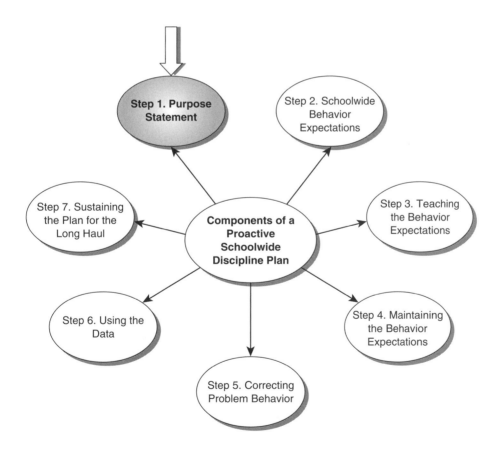

Every school or district typically has a statement that encapsulates its spirit and approach to teaching and learning. This statement serves as a cornerstone for its policy and procedures, activities, decisions, and way of doing business. The purpose of the schoolwide discipline plan is to establish and maintain student behavior that allows the accomplishment of school goals. In this sense, discipline serves as an instrument that enables teachers and students to engage in the learning process necessary to bring about the desired academic and social outcomes. For example, many schoolwide discipline plans are designed to establish student behaviors and supportive organizational structures that ensure an environment conducive to teaching and learning. This purpose emphasizes keeping student disruptions to a minimum and establishing predictable schedules so that effective teaching and learning activities can be conducted and supported in a planned and cohesive manner.

The discipline plan also provides a set of procedures that enable teachers and students to work collaboratively and constructively toward solving schoolwide academic and social behavior challenges. For example, a well-designed, proactive schoolwide plan provides specific steps for establishing expected student behaviors and for responding systematically to the full range of problem behavior displayed by some students, while at the same time encouraging the desirable behaviors displayed by most students.

■ PURPOSE STATEMENT WORKSHEET

Directions: Use two steps to develop a purpose statement for your school: (a) Write the essential features you wish to capture in your statement (Appendix E: Form 5.1, Worksheet for Developing a Purpose Statement), and (b) write these features into one or two sentences as a paragraph either in narrative style (Appendix F: Form 5.2, Purpose Statement in Narrative Style) or leave the purpose statement as a number of points (Appendix G: Form 5.3, Purpose Statement in Point Style). Examples are provided for each of these steps in Boxes 5.1, 5.2, and 5.3, and the corresponding blank forms are located in the Appendices (Appendices E, F, and G, respectively).

■ SUMMARY

The first step in developing a proactive schoolwide discipline plan is to formulate a purpose statement. This step is important for two reasons. In the first place, the step starts the process of the faculty working together, resulting in a clear product. Moreover, it is likely that this step will enable the faculty to generate a product relatively smoothly, as the content typically is not very controversial (compared to later topics, such as what consequences should be used for students who misbehave). The faculty should experience success fairly quickly. Second, the purpose statement sets the stage and the tone for the whole plan. The purpose statement is normally upbeat, constructive, student centered, and success oriented, which serves as a theme for the entire process and product. Finally, caution must be taken to ensure the language used in the purpose statement is understandable to the school community, especially students and parents.

BOX 5.1   Example of a Completed Worksheet for Developing a Schoolwide Purpose Statement

Directions:

Make a list of the ideas you would like to see included in your purpose statement.

The ideas to be included in the purpose statement of the schoolwide discipline plan at Cougar School are:

1. We have to make a commitment.

2. We must work together.

3. The school needs to be safe.

4. Everyone needs to know how it all works.

5. The result must assist student learning.

6. There must be an atmosphere of cooperation and trust.

BOX 5.2 Example of a Purpose Statement in Narrative Form Generated From Items in Box 5.1

Directions:

Use the points in Form 5.1 to generate a purpose statement in narrative style.

The purpose of the schoolwide discipline plan at Cougar School is:

We, the staff and students at Cougar Elementary School, commit ourselves to working together to provide a positive, safe, and predictable school environment that encourages learning, cooperation, and respect.

BOX 5.3   Example of a Purpose Statement in Point Style

At Pinehurst High School, students and staff will:

1. Place highest value on academic, social, and personal success;

2. Strive for proactive and safe learning and teaching environments;

3. Foster partnerships with students, families, and communities; and

4. Emphasize what works.

6

Step 2.
Schoolwide
Behavior
Expectations

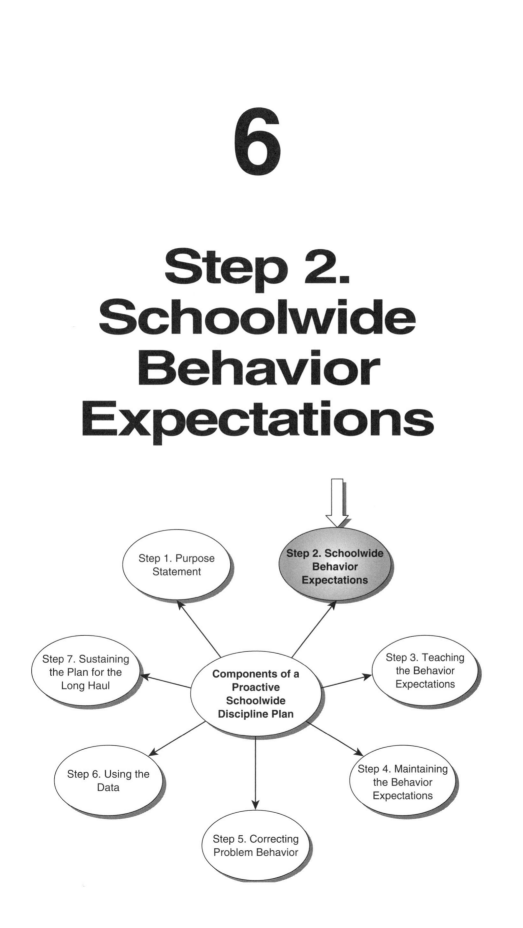

One of the most undisputed beliefs regarding teaching and learning is the strong relationship between staff expectations and student achievement and social behavior (Evertson, Emmer, Clements, & Worsham, 1994; Kauffman, Mostert, Trent, & Hallahan, 1998; Sprick, Garrison, & Howard, 1998; Walker, Colvin, & Ramsey, 1995; Wong & Wong, 1991). Simply put, if the staff expect students to achieve and behave appropriately, they will. Conversely, if the staff expect the students to underachieve and behave inappropriately, they will.

Effective development and implementation of this chapter is central to the success of the proactive schoolwide discipline plan. If these desirable expectations are solidly in place, there is less chance of problem behavior taking control of the school.

Schoolwide behavior expectations define desirable behaviors or actions of students that facilitate the teaching and learning process and the efficient operation of the schoolwide discipline plan. When students consistently display these expectations throughout the school, we can conclude that the purpose statement is being fulfilled and that the stage is set for the school to accomplish its academic and social behavior goals.

It is important to note that the proactive approach to schoolwide discipline by definition focuses on behavior that is desirable. For example, in addressing common problem behaviors, schools should endeavor to develop and maintain the desirable behaviors. If harassment is a relatively common problem behavior, the desirable behavior to be emphasized would be showing respect for one another or displaying tolerance of diversity.

Once the schoolwide expectations have been identified, the next step is to apply these expectations to the major common settings throughout the school. Typically, these settings include classrooms, hallways, buses, the cafeteria, the gymnasium, the playground, parking lots, restrooms, and locker rooms.

In this chapter, procedures are described for developing schoolwide behavior in two steps: (a) developing schoolwide behavior expectations, and (b) applying schoolwide behavior expectations to major common areas in the school. The procedures include guidelines, examples, and worksheet forms (located in the appendices).

■ DEVELOPING SCHOOLWIDE BEHAVIOR EXPECTATIONS

Guidelines for Selecting Schoolwide Behavior Expectations

The following guidelines should be followed when identifying and stating the schoolwide behavioral expectations:

1. Limit the number of behavioral expectations to no more than four or five.

2. State the behavioral expectations in positive, action-based terms using simple, understandable language as briefly as possible.

3. Identify specific behaviors to illustrate the full range of applications covering all school settings.

4. Identify specific behaviors to illustrate the range of acceptable variations and limits.

5. Establish a process for identifying behavioral expectations. Essentially, the leadership team develops a draft that is then taken to the faculty for discussion, revision as appropriate, and adoption.

6. Ensure the language used in the expectations is age appropriate for the students.

7. Ensure the expectations can be applied to academic and social behavioral outcomes.

8. Ensure the expectations are as independent from each other as possible. That is, the expectations do not overlap or say the same thing in different ways.

In Box 6.1, some examples of schoolwide expectations are presented for elementary, middle, and high school levels, respectively.

Use the blank worksheet, Appendix H: Form 6.1, Worksheet for Schoolwide Expectations, to develop your schoolwide behavior expectations. Be sure to follow the guidelines listed here for this step.

BOX 6.1   Examples of Schoolwide Expectations

Cougar Elementary Schoolwide Behavioral Expectations

1. Be respectful
2. Be cooperative
3. Be safe
4. Be kind
5. Be peaceful

Mountain Hills Middle School

All staff and students at Mountain Hills Middle School are expected to be:

1. Respectful to self and others
2. Ready to learn
3. Responsible

Pinehurst High School

1. To provide a safe and orderly environment for learning
2. To cooperate with others
3. To act responsibly
4. To respect the rights and property of others

■ APPLYING SCHOOLWIDE BEHAVIOR EXPECTATIONS TO MAJOR COMMON AREAS IN THE SCHOOL

Typically, all students spend some time of their school day in the common settings (such as the library, cafeteria, classroom, hallways, and playground). Consequently, they need clear guidelines or rules on how to behave in each of these different settings. Historically, schools had specific rules for each setting. This means that staff members had to remember the rules for each setting and do their best to ensure the students kept the rules. The value of the approach in this book of applying the schoolwide expectations to each setting is efficiency and simplicity. For example, if a schoolwide expectation is, "Be responsible," then an example of being responsible in the classroom would be to come to class prepared, hallways would be walking quietly, and the restroom would be to leave the area clean. Essentially, there is the common theme of "being responsible" with specific applications related to the proper functioning for each setting. When each schoolwide behavior expectation is applied to the common settings in the school, a matrix is formed that becomes the focus for establishing expected behavior in all settings in the school.

There are three steps in developing a schoolwide matrix for the behavior expectations applied to the common settings: (a) Identify the major common school settings, (b) develop a matrix applying the schoolwide expectations to the distinct needs of each setting, and (c) isolate the specific behaviors for each setting for separate posting and teaching as needed. An example for each of these steps is provided in Boxes 6.2, 6.3, and 6.4. Blank forms for identifying the common settings in the school and developing the schoolwide behavior matrix are located in the Appendices (Appendix I: Form 6.2, List of Major Common Settings in the School and Appendix J: Form 6.3, Common Settings Behavioral Expectations Matrix, respectively).

BOX 6.2	Example of a List of Common Settings in a Susitna Elementary School

1. Bus

2. Hallway

3. Cafeteria

4. Classroom

5. Restroom

6. Playground

SOURCE: Courtesy of Anchorage School District.

BOX 6.3   Example of a Schoolwide Behavior Expectations Matrix

Schoolwide Expectations Matrix

"A diverse community committed to the success of all learners as they become knowledgeable, responsible, and caring citizens."

Schoolwide Expectations

	Bus	Hallway	Cafeteria	Classroom	Restroom	Playground
Be Safe	• Remain seated • Listen to the driver • Walk–don't run to the bus	• Walk–don't run • Stay to the right • Keep your eyes forward	• Stay seated until dismissed • Walk–don't run • Report spills	• Push chair in • Walk–don't run	• Wash hands and use soap after using the restroom • Walk–don't run	• Use equipment appropriately • No rough play
Be Respectful	• Wait your turn • Keep hands, feet, and objects to yourself • Follow directions	• Walk in a straight line • Hands at your sides • No talking	• Use an indoor voice • Eat politely and quietly • Respond to quiet signal • Listen to the speaker	• Follow directions the first time • Be a good listener • Say please and thank you	• Wait your turn • Be patient • Be quiet • Clean up after yourself	• Follow directions the first time • Take turns
Be Responsible	• Use inside voice • Keep your stuff with you • Be a model for all students	• Have a pass at all times • Go directly to your destination • Put things away properly	• Clean up after yourself • Ask for permission when you need to get up	• Use time wisely • Put things away • Care for school property	• Flush the toilet before you leave • Report problems to your teacher • No playing	• Line up when the bell rings • Collect your things • Return equipment
Be Friendly and Caring	• Smile and greet others • Help others	• Smile • Give a nonverbal greeting	• Smile • Say please and thank you • Make friendly table talk	• Smile • Include others	• Be polite	• Smile • Share equipment • Include others

SOURCE: Courtesy of Anchorage School District.

BOX 6.4   Example of Cafeteria Expectations

Be Safe

Stay seated until dismissed

Walk–don't run

Report spills

Be Respectful

Use indoor voice

Eat politely and quietly

Respond to quiet signal

Listen to the speaker

Be Responsible

Clean up after yourself

Ask for permission when you need to get up

Be Friendly and Caring

Smile

Say please and thank you

Make friendly table talk

SOURCE: Courtesy of Anchorage School District.

■ SUMMARY

The defining feature of a proactive schoolwide discipline plan is the focus on the schoolwide behavior expectations. That is, the overall emphasis becomes establishing the behaviors we want the students to display versus the traditional focus on eliminating undesirable behavior. This is not to say that undesirable behavior is ignored or not addressed (these behaviors are fully addressed in Chapter 9, "Correcting Problem Behavior"). Rather it is a question of the primary focus which is to promote and establish expected behavior on a schoolwide basis.

These expected behaviors are universal in that students are required to exhibit them in all settings and at all times. The expected behaviors should be few in number and have ready application to all settings in the school.

7

Step 3. Teaching the Behavior Expectations

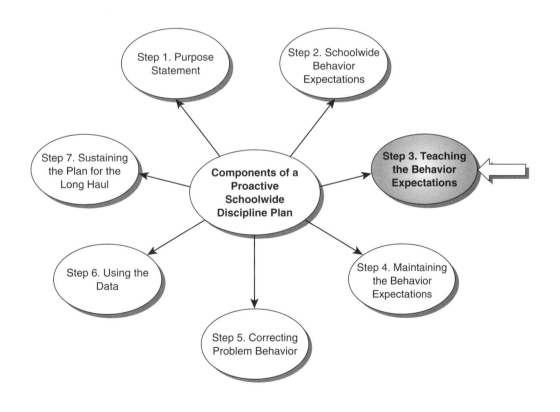

At the heart of the proactive approach to establishing discipline in this book is the position that the schoolwide behavior expectations are a set of skills that need to be taught to the students. In effect, the same teaching principles and strategies employed to provide instruction for academic, sport, and social skills are used to teach the schoolwide expectations (see Chapter 2). Cotton (1995), in an extensive review of research on effective practices for establishing schoolwide discipline, highlighted the critical role of teaching behavior with the finding that "children below fourth grade require a great deal of instruction and practice in classroom rules and procedures . . . effective management, especially in the early grades is more an instructional than a disciplinary enterprise" (p. 8).

Similar findings were also reported for older students (Grades 4–12), showing strong positive results were obtained by using a teaching approach: "With older students, researchers have noted that the best results are obtained through vigilantly reminding students about the rules and procedures and monitoring their compliance with them" (Cotton, 1995, p. 8). In addition to providing reminders and supervision, Colvin, Kame'enui, and Sugai (1993) found that including the instructional component of providing feedback also significantly assisted in teaching older students (Grades 4–12) classroom expectations. In this chapter, operational details for teaching the schoolwide behavior expectations to the students are described for younger students (K–3) and older students (Grades 4–12).

■ TEACHING BEHAVIOR EXPECTATIONS TO YOUNGER STUDENTS (K–3)

Using a generic instructional plan for teaching behavior with a wide range of applications has been well documented in research and best practice (Colvin & Lazar, 1997; Darch & Kame'enui, 2003; Simon Weinstein, 2003; Sprick, Garrison, & Howard, 1998). Instructional approaches have been used to establish expected behavior on a schoolwide basis, in classrooms, and with students who display chronic problem behavior (Colvin, 2004; Colvin et al., 1993; OSEP Center on Positive and Behavioral Interventions and Supports, 2004; Sugai, 1996).

In teaching expected behavior to younger students in Grades K through 3, the following five steps are recommended to develop behavior instruction plans: (a) explain, (b) specify student behaviors, (c) practice, (d) monitor, and (e) review.

Step 1: Explain

Provide adequate reasons and purposes for the particular behavior. Encourage the students' participation as much as possible in developing the rationale for the behavior expectations. Make sure that the students understand what you require of them and why you require it.

Step 2: Specify Student Behaviors

Clearly specify the behaviors that are required of the students. These behaviors should be discrete, sequential, and observable, as well as expressed in words that the children can understand.

Step 3: Practice

Practice is essential for developing fluency in all skill areas such as reading, math, music, or athletic skills. To provide adequate practice on behavior expectations, teachers need to design practice activities, schedule practice sessions, and most important, ensure all students have an opportunity to demonstrate and practice the expected behavior.

Step 4: Monitor

Provide students with opportunities to exhibit the behaviors independently in real situations. Carefully monitor the students' performance, especially in the early stages. Provide feedback to the students on their performance at the completion of the activity. Use the monitoring information to determine if the students need more practice.

Step 5: Review

Develop a system to periodically review the students' performance on the expected behaviors. Include formal observation of the students' behavior to assess how many of the students are following the expected behaviors, how long the demonstrations are taking, and what kinds of problem behavior arise. If problem behavior occurs, briefly introduce Steps 1, 3, and 4 (explain, practice, and monitor) before the next opportunity to demonstrate the expected behaviors. Remember to strongly acknowledge cooperation.

A sample behavior instruction plan is presented in Box 7.1 for teaching behavior expectations in the hallways. Use the worksheet, Appendix K: Form 7.1, Instruction Plan for Teaching a Schoolwide Expectation, for developing behavior instruction plans for each of the schoolwide behavior expectations and corresponding settings. It is strongly recommended that all teachers target expected behaviors and settings at the same time. In this way, the students receive the same message throughout the school. Once the expected behaviors have been taught, the next step is to use maintenance procedures described in the next section.

TEACHING BEHAVIOR EXPECTATIONS TO OLDER STUDENTS (GRADES 4–12) AND A MAINTENANCE TEACHING PLAN FOR YOUNGER STUDENTS

The instruction plan for students in fourth grade through twelfth grade and the maintenance teaching plan for younger students (once the behavior has been taught using the five-step procedure described previously) is the same. This procedure involves three steps: (a) remind, (b) supervise, and (c) provide feedback. An illustration of this teaching plan for secondary students is presented in Box 7.2, and the corresponding blank form is located in Appendix L: Form 7.2, Teaching Behavior Expectations to Older Students and a Maintenance Plan for Younger Students.

BOX 7.1	Illustration of a Behavior Instruction Plan for Younger Students

Cougar Elementary School

Expected Behavior: Be Responsible

Common Setting: Hallways

Step 1: Explain

☐ Avoid disturbing others

☐ Avoid injury

☐ Save time

Step 2: Specify student behaviors

☐ Walk

☐ Keep hands, feet, and objects to self

☐ Be silent (no talking unless directed by the teacher)

☐ Stay on right side of hallway

☐ Keep in line

☐ Keep up with the group

Step 3: Practice

☐ Role play in the classroom

☐ Actually practice in the hallway

☐ Have regular practices (once or twice each term, when there are problems, and as booster sessions before or after breaks)

☐ Provide frequent reminders

Step 4: Monitor

☐ Vary your position (front, back, and middle of line)

☐ Scan the whole line

☐ Interact with the students

☐ Reinforce, remind, and correct student behavior

Step 5: Review

☐ Give the students feedback (praise appropriate behavior and identify problems)

☐ Solicit student feedback: "How did we do on keeping in line today?"

☐ Deliver consequences as necessary

BOX 7.2   Illustration of a Behavior Instruction Plan for Older Students

Silverglen Middle School

Schoolwide Behavior Expectation: Be responsible

Common Setting: Hallways (transitioning between classrooms)

Specific Behaviors: Be on time for class and behave appropriately in the hallways

---

Remind: Explain to the students that they need to behave appropriately in the hallways and get to class on time. Point out that it is OK to chat but hanging out to chat is not acceptable, that is, they need to keep moving. The expected behaviors are: (a) Keep the noise down, (b) use appropriate language, and (c) keep moving. Provide these reminders just before the end of the period when the students are about to exit the classroom. The expectations are also read during the morning announcements on the address system.

Supervise: All staff are asked to position themselves near the doorway, or even a little out in the hallway, so that they can observe the students' behavior and so the students can see them. Use prompts to keep the students moving as needed, and use this opportunity to greet the students as they come to class.

Provide Feedback: Conduct a brief discussion at the start of the period on how the students cooperated with the expectations (keep the noise down, use appropriate language, and keep moving). Acknowledge the students who were on time for class and who cooperated with the three expectations. Provide some indicators as to whether the class is doing better or worse each day.

SUMMARY ■

At the heart of a proactive schoolwide discipline plan is the notion that expected behavior needs to be taught. Simply put, "If you want good behavior, you have to teach it." In this model, the way to teach expected behavior is the same as the methods used to teach any skill, whether it is academics, sports, or music. The overall approach for establishing expected behavior in a school is to use the same teaching principles and steps for teaching any skill. The basic assumption is that desirable behavior has to be learned, which implies that it has to be taught.

Behavior instruction plans were presented depicting the teaching steps involved in targeting the schoolwide behavior expectations. Adaptations for these plans were described and illustrated for elementary and secondary students.

The overall power of this approach for establishing expected behavior is that it is based on an instructional model. This means that it is very compatible with the training and approaches teachers take to help their students learn other skills.

8

Step 4. Maintaining the Behavior Expectations

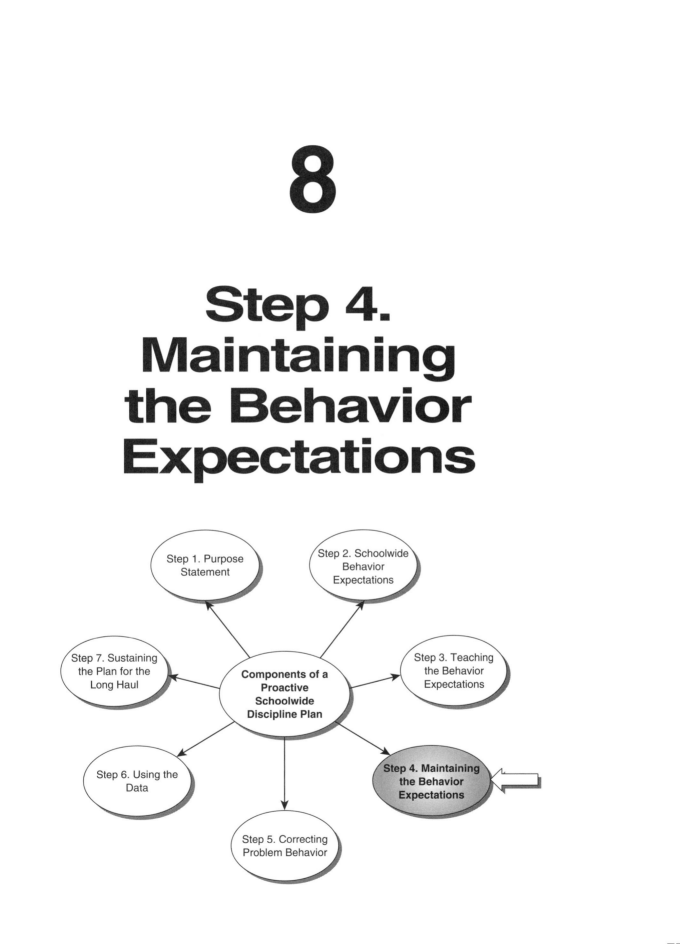

Once the schoolwide expectations have been taught and systematically applied to common settings throughout the school (school-wide matrix), additional steps need to be taken to assist the students to exhibit the expected behaviors on a consistent basis over time. If these steps are not taken, it is highly likely that some, if not many, students will discontinue displaying these behaviors, and problem behavior will likely emerge. Several writers who have worked extensively in the field have stressed that schools must engage in specific activities in an ongoing manner to sustain these schoolwide behaviors following initial teaching (Colvin, Kame'enui, & Sugai, 1993; Lewis & Sugai, 1999; Sprick, Sprick, & Garrison, 1992; Wong & Wong, 1991). In this chapter, two steps are recommended for sustaining schoolwide expected behaviors: (a) modeling by faculty through informal practices and (b) schoolwide recognition plans.

■ MODELING BY FACULTY THROUGH INFORMAL PRACTICES

Students are very astute observers of adult behavior. Consequently, an important key in determining whether students buy into maintaining the schoolwide behavior expectations is their perception of the behavior of the faculty. If the faculty serve as good role models for the students, there is much more likelihood that the students will maintain their behavior. There are a number of practices for faculty to engage in that will increase the likelihood that students will maintain their efforts with the schoolwide expectations.

Act as Role Models for Good Behavior. The faculty serves as significant role models for their students when they show respect and courtesy to their students, encourage their students, solve problems in a calm and respectful manner, show empathy and concern for their students when needed, and are firm, fair, and consistent. In general, the faculty must serve as a model to their students for the schoolwide behavior expectations.

Show Respect and Courtesy to Each Other. One of the best ways to demonstrate expected behavior to students is for staff to exhibit these same behaviors to each other at a faculty level, such as solving problems in a calm and respectful manner, showing consideration to each other, and exhibiting polite manners to each other.

Continually Emphasize Positive Aspects of the Discipline Plan. Positive approaches are very effective for establishing behavioral expectations and creating a welcoming and supportive school environment. To this end, staff should frequently acknowledge students who demonstrate expected behavior; use positive and proactive procedures; show interest in the students; show concern for their well-being; provide constant reminders, supervision, and feedback on the behavioral expectations; and place strong emphasis on self-directed student behavior.

Solicit Student Input and Involvement. The building team and faculty should take opportunities to involve the student body in leadership roles and management as appropriate such as using the student council, facilitating schoolwide social activities and events, and conducting peer-helper programs.

SCHOOLWIDE RECOGNITION PLANS ■

The purpose of schoolwide recognition plans is to acknowledge and show appreciation to students who have provided positive demonstrations of the schoolwide behavioral expectations. In this way, the faculty is providing attention to the students who display the desired behaviors. These plans may also function as incentives for students who do not exhibit the schoolwide expectations on a regular basis.

Generally, it is very important for the leadership team to do some groundwork with the faculty before these plans are undertaken. The reason is that some staff members may oppose these plans for the following reasons: "Why should we reward students for what they should be doing anyway?" or "We shouldn't have to bribe kids to do the right thing." The overall response to these concerns is that students need recognition and respond positively to acts of appreciation. Staff must emphasize that the focus is to show appreciation to the students versus simply distributing awards.

In developing schoolwide recognition plans, it is very important to have some awards that are accessible to *all* students. Moreover, it is crucial for the leadership team to take responsibility for coordinating the particular award process. Otherwise, the various logistical steps may not get completed, and the plans will lose their effectiveness.

There are a number of factors that need to be addressed when developing a schoolwide recognition plan. These factors are listed in Box 8.1. A sample schoolwide recognition plan is presented in Box 8.2, and the corresponding blank form is located in the Appendices (Appendix M: Form 8.1, Schoolwide Recognition Matrix).

BOX 8.1   Factors to Be Considered in Developing a Schoolwide Recognition Plan

- Specify the specific schoolwide behavioral expectation to be acknowledged.
- Give the award a title.
- Define eligibility criteria.
- Determine where and when the award is presented.
- Identify a staff member to coordinate the award process.
- Determine what the actual award is (specifically, what is presented to the student).
- Decide on a dissemination procedure, that is, how the recognition is displayed or communicated to others.
- Determine the frequency of distribution.
- Develop a summary matrix for the various recognition plans.

BOX 8.2 Illustration of a Schoolwide Recognition Matrix: Aurora Middle School

Name	Achievement Criteria	Award	Presented at…	Frequency	Number of Awards Per Year	Type	Coordinated by	Dissemination
Caught in the Act	Following behavior expectations in any setting	Verbal praise Tickets	May be received anywhere on campus except student's own classroom Recognized by classroom teacher Recognized at home	Daily	Undetermined for individuals Twice yearly for classes	Individual Group	Ms. Smith Mrs. Johnson	Half of ticket goes home with each student Between classes competition for an ice cream party (twice yearly)
Academic Excellence Award	Marked improvement or Best effort or Maximum academic achievement	Certificate of recognition	Special school assembly	Monthly	One student per classroom each month	Individual	Ms. Bush Mr. Har	Home School newsletter Bulletin board in school hallway with photos Community announcements
Superstar	More than 25 tickets earned in a quarter Meets academic excellence criteria	Gift certificate School T-shirt	Special school assembly	Quarterly	Two students per classroom each term (quarter)	Individual	Ms. Smith Mr. Jones	School newsletter Home Community announcements
Classwide Attendance Award	Perfect attendance (except excused)	Pizza party	Special school assembly	Twice yearly	Two	Class	Mr. Haden Mr. Kent	School newsletter Home Community announcements
Individual Attendance Award	Perfect attendance (except excused)	Gift certificate Bumper sticker	Special school assembly	Once each year	Undetermined	Individual	Mrs. Kim Mr. Hope	School newsletter Home Community announcements

SUMMARY ■

It is generally accepted among educators that students need to be recognized and appreciated. However, administrators are very familiar with the constraint that they spend a great deal of their time with students who exhibit problem behavior. Consequently, they have the concern that the students who keep the rules, cooperate with the expectations, and behave appropriately at school receive very little of their time. By having a schoolwide recognition plan, the students who consistently exhibit the schoolwide behavior expectations receive recognition and attention for their efforts. Moreover, these plans are one of the surest strategies for ensuring that the desirable schoolwide behaviors are sustained.

Educators must also realize that their own behavior toward the students and each other is a powerful tool for demonstrating the schoolwide behavior expectations. Finally, the effectiveness of these plans will be largely determined by the willingness of the team and faculty to attend to the details of implementation with high consistency.

9

Step 5. Correcting Problem Behavior

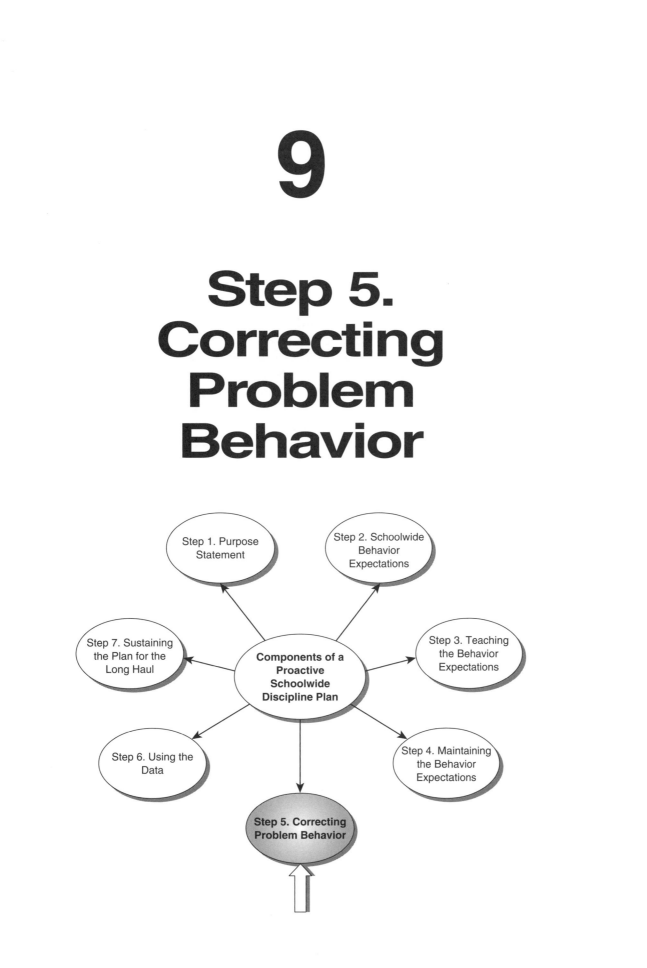

Step 1. Purpose Statement

Step 2. Schoolwide Behavior Expectations

Step 7. Sustaining the Plan for the Long Haul

Components of a Proactive Schoolwide Discipline Plan

Step 3. Teaching the Behavior Expectations

Step 6. Using the Data

Step 4. Maintaining the Behavior Expectations

Step 5. Correcting Problem Behavior

This particular chapter on addressing problem behavior, in the author's opinion, is one of the hardest to implement effectively in schools. The reason is that there has been a long history in education that problem behavior needs to be punished and if the problem behavior recurs, then we need to deliver stronger punishment. It can easily lead to a student infraction–punishment cycle. The prevalence of this practice was addressed more fully in Chapter 2.

However, a primary underpinning of a proactive approach to school-wide discipline is that when problem behavior occurs, more can be done besides delivering negative consequences. It is important to assist the student to behave appropriately in the future. To accomplish this goal, an instructional approach is used to correct problem behavior.

When errors occur during instruction, two steps are usually taken by teachers: (a) Feedback is provided that an error has occurred, and (b) extra steps are taken to ensure that the student has the appropriate skills to perform the task correctly in the future. For example, if a student makes an error in math, the teacher lets the student know with feedback like, "Oops, we have a wrong answer here. We must have made a mistake somewhere." The second step involves providing assistance so that the student corrects the problem. A number of correction options are typically used, such as that the teacher may ask the student to do the problem again, stating the steps used. This information enables the teacher to pinpoint where the error occurs. The teacher could have a volunteer do the problem on the board if a number of students made an error. The teacher may back up a little and restate the steps involved and then provide the student with more practice examples. Also, the teacher may ask the students to check with their neighbors. Finally, the teacher checks whether the students can remember how to perform the task by presenting similar questions in a later lesson. In effect, when an error occurs, the teacher usually informs the student that an error has occurred and then takes steps to ensure that the student learns how to perform the task correctly both in the present lesson and in later lessons.

It is this second step of providing additional assistance to the student to ensure appropriate behavior in the future that is difficult to implement in many schools when it comes to addressing problem behavior.

The basic approach for addressing problem behavior is to apply the same two steps used in instruction to correct errors: (a) Logical and appropriate consequences are delivered to provide students with feedback that unacceptable behavior has occurred, and (b) specific strategies are used to ensure that the students learn the expected behaviors. In other words, a problem-solving approach is used to correct problem behavior.

In a proactive model to effectively correct problem behavior, the following procedures will be described: (a) a system involving a continuum of responses for the full range of problem behavior, (b) systematic procedures for managing office referrals, and (c) systematic procedures for managing problem behavior that may not warrant office referrals.

A SYSTEM INVOLVING A CONTINUUM OF RESPONSES FOR THE FULL RANGE OF PROBLEM BEHAVIOR

Many could recognize this situation: Two students are sitting outside the principal's office. One student received an office referral for not having a pencil in class, while the other student was referred for stabbing another student with a pencil. Each student waits his or her turn to report to the principal. The point is that the student who stabbed another student with a pencil exhibited very serious behavior and should have been sent to the office. However, the other student, who exhibited a relatively minor problem behavior—not having a pencil for class—should have been dealt with by the teacher in the classroom.

Schools need to have a system in place in which the full range of problem behavior can be addressed, from relatively low-level behavior such as side talk in class to serious problem behavior such as assault. This is not to say that the relatively minor behavior is not to be addressed. Rather, it is to say that these behaviors should be managed directly in the context where they occur and that the more serious behavior may need administrative intervention through an office referral. In other words, a system needs to be developed in which a continuum of responses is available to address the full range of problem behavior that is likely to occur in a public school. Figure 9.1 presents an example of a system designed to address the full range of problem behavior.

Figure 9.1   Continuum of Responses to the Full Range of Student Behavior

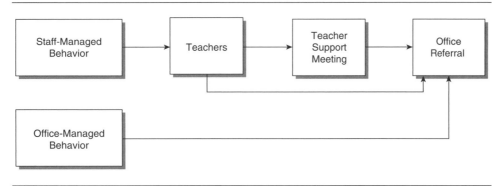

OVERVIEW OF CONTINUUM OF RESPONSES FOR ADDRESSING PROBLEM BEHAVIOR

In Figure 9.1, the continuum begins with making a clear distinction between which behaviors warrant direct office referrals and which should be managed by staff, usually in the context where the behavior occurs. Behaviors warranting office referrals need to be clearly listed. These behaviors usually involve follow-up by an administrator, typically resulting in some kind of action drawn from an array of negative consequences; some restitution activity may be required, and strategies may be raised to help the student deal with these situations more effectively in the future. This process will be described more fully later in this chapter.

The remainder of the continuum of responses to the full range of student behavior refers to the lower level or lower intensity behaviors. These behaviors refer to the branch of the continuum in Figure 9.1 listed as Staff-Managed Behavior (as distinct from the more serious behavior listed as Office-Managed Behavior in the diagram). Just because these behaviors do not warrant office referrals, it is still important that these behaviors are addressed effectively, otherwise they can become chronic and seriously disrupt the teaching-learning process.

The first step in this branch of the continuum for staff-managed behavior is for the teacher or adult supervisor (such as a teacher assistant at recess or study hall) to use best practice strategies for correcting these behaviors. If the problem behavior persists, the next step involves addressing the behavior at a teacher support meeting. This meeting needs to be brief and very focused. It usually consists of a few teachers gathering on a regular basis, such as a grade-level meeting at which one of the agenda items is recurring problem behavior. The basic approach in these meetings is for the teachers to brainstorm ideas on how to manage the problem behavior. This process will be described more fully later in the chapter.

If the problem behavior persists following implementation of suggestions by other teachers, then the student is referred to the office. The assumption is that the teachers and supervisors have done what they can individually and collectively to correct the problem and have not been successful. By making an office referral at this juncture, the student receives information that the recurring problem behavior is serious enough to warrant intervention by the school administration.

The steps in the continuum for responding to the full range of problem behavior will now be described.

■ OFFICE-MANAGED BEHAVIOR

Cotton (1995), in an extensive review of effective school discipline plans, concluded that the most divisive issue between staff and the administration is what behaviors warrant office referrals and what happens following an office referral. It is crucial for staff to carefully develop an office-referral system in which these issues are effectively addressed.

There are five steps in developing a schoolwide office-referral system: (a) list the behaviors warranting an office referral, (b) clearly define each of the behaviors on the office-referral list, (c) construct a functional office-referral form, (d) develop procedures for staff to follow in making a referral, and (e) ensure that the office (usually administration) has capacity to meet the range of problems that may be referred.

Step 1: Define Behaviors Warranting Office Referrals

These behaviors typically include serious disruption, behavior affecting safety, and potentially illegal behavior. In most cases, the school district policy dictates a list of behaviors warranting office referrals. It is assumed that behaviors not on this list would be classified as staff-managed behavior.

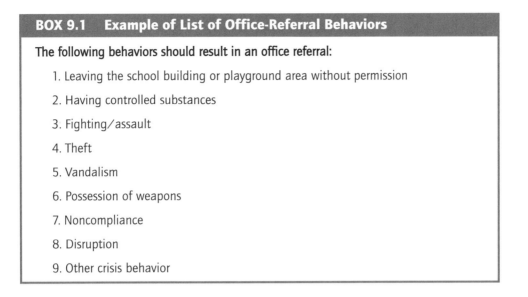

A sample list is presented in Box 9.1, and the corresponding blank form is located in the Appendices (Appendix N: Form 9.1, Worksheet for Office-Referral Behaviors).

Step 2: Clearly Define Each of the Behaviors on the Office-Referral List

Once staff have reached agreement on the list of behaviors that should result in an office referral, the next step is to develop written definitions for each of these behaviors. The definitions will help staff to be consistent in assessing whether an office referral should be made. Otherwise, without the definitions, staff will have different interpretations of what the behavior means. The definitions also assist in follow-up communication with the students and parents. In Step 3, this model recommends that the definitions be printed on the back of the office-referral form.

An illustration of definitions developed at a school is presented in Box 9.2, and the corresponding blank form is located in the Appendices (Appendix O: Form 9.2, Worksheet for Office-Referral Behavior Definitions).

Step 3: Construct a Functional Office-Referral Form

Basically, when a staff member makes an office referral, the problem is given to the administration to manage. Consequently, it is critical for the administration to receive adequate information so that the situation can be processed. The office-referral form needs to be designed to meet the following needs:

- Provide the administration with the critical information to process the problem.
- Contain sufficient information to provide a source for adequate communication with the students involved and other parties as appropriate such as parents, law enforcement, and other agencies.
- Allow for data entry into a computer record system (Chapter 10).
- Enable trends to be determined, such as locations, times of day, specific behaviors, and patterns with certain students and staff.

BOX 9.2	Illustration of Office-Referral Behavior Definitions

Meredith Elementary School

Write an office referral when these problems occur.

Problem Behavior	Definition
1. Leaving the school building or playground area without permission	Leaving the building, classroom, or assigned area without obtaining prior approval of the teacher or administrator.
2. Having controlled substances	Being in possession of or using any form of alcohol, drugs, or tobacco. The term *drug* includes all mood-altering substances or facsimile thereof that have not been medically prescribed for the student.
3. Fighting/assault	Fighting involves the exchange of mutual physical contact, such as pushing, shoving, and hitting with or without injury. Assault refers to behavior in which one student or group of students may be inflicting bodily harm to another student or staff member.
4. Theft	Taking property belonging to the school or any individual or group without prior permission.
5. Vandalism	Intentionally causing damage to or defacing school property or the property of others.
6. Weapons	Being in possession of any items designated as weapons, including simulated weapons. Weapons are defined to include, but not limited to, noxious gases (such as mace), knives, chains, clubs, brass knuckles, black-jacks, and firearms.
7. Noncompliance	Refusing to follow directions when reasonable efforts have been made to enable the student to cooperate.
8. Disruption	Having sustained, disruptive behavior that prevents instruction from continuing or continuing with difficulty after reasonable attempts have been made to correct the behavior.
9. Other crisis behavior	Having serious low-incident behavior that affects safety or is regarded as crisis or emergency behavior.

- Track consequences or action taken.
- An illustration of an office-referral form from a local middle school that captures these features is presented in Box 9.3.

Step 4: Develop Steps for Staff to Follow in Making a Referral

Once again, it is very important for a school to develop very clear procedures for making an office referral and to follow the procedures consistently. The following guidelines are recommended:

BOX 9.3   Sydney Middle School Office-Referral Form

Student _____   Grade 6 7 8 Date _____

Referred by _____   Homeroom Teacher _____

Reason for Referral

☐ Repeated Minor Infraction(s)

    ☐ Documentation Attached

    ☐ Parent Contacted

☐ Serious School Violation

    ☐ Attendance

    ☐ Controlled Substance(s)

    ☐ Defiance

    ☐ Discrimination, Harassment, Hazing

    ☐ Dress Code

    ☐ Fighting, Assault

    ☐ Off-Campus Violation

    ☐ Serious Disruption

    ☐ Theft

    ☐ Vandalism

    ☐ Verbal Abuse

    ☐ Weapon(s)

    ☐ Other _____

Incident Report

Specify times, places, those involved, relevant conditions and initial steps to address problem.

_____

_____

_____

_____

_____

_____

_____

_____

_____

_____

_____

_____

_____

_____

Location

☐ Recess   ☐ Hallway

☐ Classroom ☐ Gymnasium

☐ Cafeteria ☐ Bus Stop

☐ Library   ☐ Bus

☐ Media Center

☐ Other _____

Action taken by administrator or designee

☐ Conference with student

☐ Parent contacted (phone/note)

☐ Student suspended _____days

☐ Referred to school behavior support team

☐ Principal's hearing for possible expulsion _____

☐ Conference requested with teacher and student

☐ Parent conference requested

☐ Student placed on detention _____days

☐ Community service

☐ Police contacted

☐ Lane County Youth Services contacted

☐ Other _____

Administrator's Comments

_____

_____

_____

_____

_____

_____

_____

_____

_____

_____

_____

_____ _____

Administrator's Signature   Date

Routing

White: Office   Yellow: Parent

Pink: Homeroom Teacher Gold: Referring Staff

To Parent or Guardian: This is a copy of an official referral for your son or daughter made by a staff member of Sydney Middle School, 8998 Snell Blvd., Eugene, Oregon 97435. The action taken is indicated.

    Please sign and return or call 387-8856 to indicate receipt.

_____   _____

Parent's or Guardian's Signature   Date

1. Write an office referral only for student behaviors listed on the referral form.

2. Complete in full the details specified on the office-referral form.

3. Depending on the gravity of the problem and the state of the student:
   - send the student directly to the office,
   - take the student yourself (ensure your class is covered), or
   - call for an escort.

4. At the office, the administrator typically:
   - addresses and reviews the problem with the student beginning with the office-referral form submitted by referring staff member,
   - delivers consequences and an action plan as appropriate,
   - completes the office-referral form,
   - submits the completed form to secretary (or designee) to be entered into database, and
   - arranges to visit with the referring staff member and others as appropriate.

Step 5: Ensure That the Office (Usually Administration) Has Capacity to Meet the Range of Problems That May Be Referred

For the majority of problems that are referred to the office, the administrator or designee reviews the problem, encourages the student to reflect on the behavior, problem solves, and in most cases, delivers a consequence. However, additional levels of response may become necessary for the following behaviors:

Potentially Illegal Infractions. Here, the school needs to have clear procedures developed with local law enforcement officers, onsite officers, or campus security personnel as appropriate.

Crisis or Emergency Behavior. It is very common today for schools to form a school crisis team, whose members receive adequate training in the range of crises that may occur in the school. In addition, all staff should be clear on their role in these crises, how to access the team, how to respond while waiting for the team, and any follow-up that is needed, such as documentation.

Chronic Behavior. These behaviors are neither crises nor legal infractions. Some examples include frequent disruption, ongoing noncompliance, attendance problems, and often failing grades or unsatisfactory work. In these cases, the typical consequences and practices at the office do not change the student's behavior. Many schools now have formed a behavior support team to assist with these chronic problems. This team is trained to analyze behavior and develop highly individual interventions designed to assist students with their needs and to help them become successful in school. (Check the Positive Behavioral Interventions and Supports site, www.pbis.org, for specific details for the effective functioning of a behavior support team.)

STAFF-MANAGED BEHAVIOR   ■

Staff are expected to manage the problem behaviors that are not listed for office referrals described previously. While these behaviors are often called "minor behaviors," it is still very important that there is a systems approach for addressing and correcting these behaviors. If not, the behaviors may worsen or gradually erode the positive learning environment the teachers are trying to establish and maintain. For example, if a student does not come to class prepared and this behavior persists, then it is not long before that student may refuse to do any assigned work or participate in other class activities. In addition, other students may follow suit, and as a result, the teacher's effectiveness will be diminished.

A range of best practice procedures is always recommended for an individual teacher or staff person to manage these lower level behaviors. Staff should be expected to seize every opportunity to establish appropriate student behavior (many suggestions of such strategies are presented in Chapters 7 and 8). Behavior-management procedures should provide increased positive reinforcement for promoting expected behavior and deliver an array of negative consequences, as appropriate, based on the severity of the problem behavior.

Several schools have effectively adopted a three-step procedure for implementing a continuum of responses for staff-managed behavior: (a) response by individual staff members, (b) referral to a teacher support team meeting, and (c) referral to the office.

Step 1: Response by Individual Staff Members

At this level, staff members are expected to use their own management skills to address the problem behavior. While there are many strategies for dealing with misbehavior, the following sequence of responses are recommended to correct these kinds of behaviors.

Remove adult and peer attention from the student who is displaying inappropriate behavior and pay attention to nearby students who are exhibiting the expected behavior. For example, Sarah is talking loudly in class during an individual seatwork assignment. Her teacher turns her back to Sarah and looks at the students nearby who are working quietly. The teacher says, "Students in this row are doing a very nice job in quietly working on their assignments."

Redirect the student to the expected behavior with a gesture or verbal prompt, and intentionally acknowledge subsequent cooperation and displays of expected behavior. For example, the teacher gives Sarah a prompt by placing her finger next to her lips and saying, "Remember, Sarah, please use a quiet voice." If Sarah begins to talk quietly, the teacher says, "Thank you, Sarah."

Secure the student's attention and directly inform him or her of the expected behavior, provide immediate opportunities for practice, and acknowledge cooperation and appropriate displays of expected behavior. For example, the teacher says, "Sarah, look here please. If you wish to talk, please speak quietly, otherwise, you are disturbing the class. Now what do you need?" If Sarah responds in a quiet voice, the teacher says, "There you go, Sarah. I can easily hear you, and you are not disturbing the class."

Deliver a warning by providing an opportunity for the student to choose between the expected behavior and a penalty or loss of privilege. For example, "Sarah, look, you are asked to talk quietly, or you will have to miss some recess."

Follow through and deliver the penalty or loss of privilege (for example, loss of some recess time) immediately or at the earliest opportunity in a calm and matter-of-fact manner.

Use additional resources to address the problem if there is no improvement in the student's behavior after three or four occasions in which these steps have been followed. At this point, the issue should be raised at the next level in the continuum, the teacher support meeting.

Records and documentation of the problem and interventions used to address the problem should be developed. Staff should be in agreement on the purpose of these records, dissemination procedures, specification of problem behavior and expected behavior, and the strategies used.

Remember the Fair Pair Rule

   Whenever a student exhibits inappropriate behavior, is corrected, and then gets back on task, it is *critical* to reinforce the student for being on task at the earliest opportunity.

Step 2: Referral to a Teacher Support Team Meeting

Once a teacher has tried to correct a problem behavior in a planned manner, the next step is to refer the problem to a teacher team meeting. These meetings can be called on an informal basis or can be part of a regular meeting that teachers hold (for example, a weekly, grade-level meeting). A variety of labels have been used to name this staffing structure (for example, "teacher assistance team," "child study team," "pre-referral meeting," "behavior resource team," and "discipline team"). There are several important advantages in staff coming together to address such problem behavior in this manner:

- The meetings provide an opportunity to use the ideas of an "untapped resource," namely, other staff members.
- When teachers meet in this fashion, there is a greater likelihood of agreed-on procedures being implemented consistently.
- More intervention options can be generated in this process, which may result in fewer office referrals.
- Individual staff members receive support and assistance.
- Ongoing staff development can be facilitated.

While the concept of teacher meetings is very sound, we must keep in mind that teachers are very busy and their available time for meetings is quite limited. The following guidelines have been distilled from various attempts to effectively implement the teacher team meeting practice:

- Teacher team meetings should be called by the teacher after three or four documented incidents of the problem behavior have occurred (again, these are behaviors that are not on the list warranting an office referral).
- The teacher team meeting should be scheduled on a regular basis during ongoing staff or grade-level meetings.
- A special teacher team meeting can be called if a teacher needs more immediate assistance (with as many teachers in attendance as possible).
- A form should be developed and used to document each case and to guide the teacher team meeting activities. Box 9.4 presents an illustration of a teacher team meeting and the plan arising from this meeting. A blank form for this meeting can be found in the Appendices (Appendix P: Form 9.3, Teacher Team Meeting for Staff-Managed Behavior).

The teacher initiating the meeting should complete as much of the form as possible before the meeting so participants will have some prior information about the case. This information can also serve as a starting point for the meeting.

- A note taker and time keeper should be identified at the beginning of each meeting. It is critical to follow the agenda and stay within the allocated time lines, otherwise the meetings will drag on and teachers will be reluctant to commit to subsequent meetings.
- Problem behaviors (list no more than two) should be prioritized. Descriptions of these behaviors should be written in language that focuses on observable behavior.
- A specific, expected behavior should be paired with each problem behavior and also described in observable form.
- If possible, one to three of the least intrusive and least time-consuming strategies for establishing expected behaviors should be selected. If the expected behaviors do not occur at acceptable levels, more intrusive and time-consuming strategies should be considered.
- Although strategies for teaching expected behaviors should be given the greatest attention, responses to the problem behaviors—negative consequences—should also be addressed and determined. Again, least intrusive and least aversive criteria should always be applied in selecting negative consequences.
- A simple tracking system needs to be developed so that a quick evaluation of the plan can be determined. The team needs to know whether the plan is working. Simple frequency counts or sampling during set times is a relatively easy tracking procedure.
- Finally, a specific date should be established to review the progress of the plan in achieving anticipated outcomes. The referring teacher should have available the tracking data to help team members evaluate the plan and make decisions based on the data.

BOX 9.4   Teacher Team Meeting for Staff-Managed Behavior

☑ Behavior Problem   ☐ Academic Problem

Student Name: Brock W   Grade: 7   Date: January 24, 2007

Teacher(s): Fred J   # of Previous Behavior Reports/Staff Meeting: None

Staff Present: Sarah H; Michael S; Estella Y, Dominic P, Michelle R.

Problem Behavior(s) (2 minutes)	*Expected Behavior(s)* (2 minutes)
Brock refuses to work by himself. He always has to be talking to someone or wandering around the room. As soon as the class is asked to work on something by themselves, he has to start talking with other students. When he is isolated, he just starts walking around the room.	Brock has demonstrated several times that he is quite smart and can do the work.

Strategies to Teach Expected Behaviors (select 1–3) (3 minutes)

☑ Reminders	☐ Practice	☐ Parent contact
☑ Reinforcers	☐ Individual contacts	☐ Counseling
☑ Feedback	☐ Monitoring sheet	☐ Tutoring
☐ Contract	☐ Self-management	☐ Modified assignments
☐ Other		

Strategies to Correct Problem Behavior(s) (1 minute)

☐ Time out	☑ Parent contact
☑ Loss of privilege	☐ Detention
☐ Other	

Action Plan (5 minutes)

Who	*What*	*When*
Fred	Develop contract with Brock	Immediately
All teachers present	Check his response to working alone in their classes and report to Fred	Over next week
Estella	Visit with him	This week

Tracking System: Simple count of number of chances to work alone and percentage successful

Student Conference Date: February 15, 2007 Start Date: January 26 Review Date: February 23, 2007

Copies to: Teachers Present

Office File

Teacher: Fred J

Other: Seventh-Grade Administrator

Step 3: Referral to the Office

Once an individual teacher has used his or her best attempts to correct a problem behavior, the teacher team meetings have been used, and the problem persists, the next step is to make an office referral. In this sense, the problem behavior is deemed chronic and administrative intervention is needed. Office support is essential for chronic, minor problem behavior, otherwise staff may become discouraged, and their overall efforts may become attenuated.

In making an office referral for chronic staff-managed behavior, teachers are usually required to check off the appropriate box on the office-referral form and follow specific procedures. For example, the sample office-referral form used by Sydney Middle School, Box 9.3, breaks out the reason for an office referral into two categories, "repeated minor infractions" and "serious school violation." Moreover, this school requires that when an office referral is made for repeated minor infractions, the teacher provide written documentation (usually copies of the completed form, Appendix P: Form 9.3, Teacher Team Meeting for Staff-Managed Behavior) and contact the parent regarding the problem behavior. The administrator handling the referral now follows the usual procedures for addressing office referrals.

SUMMARY ■

There is no argument that public school personnel have to manage problem student behavior at ever-increasing levels of intensity and severity. Behavioral episodes are occurring routinely in schools across the nation that would have been unthinkable several decades ago. However, research findings on these problem behaviors suggest many practices that can be quite effective in minimizing and correcting these problems.

In this chapter, a model has been presented that has been implemented and maintained in many schools for addressing and correcting the full range of problem behavior. This model presumes that proactive strategies for preventing serious and chronic problem behavior are viable, user friendly, effective, and cost efficient. It is recognized that this schoolwide model for correcting problem behavior is basically a universal intervention that may have little to no effect on correcting the behavior of a few students with highly challenging behavior. In such instances, more intensive, selected, and individualized interventions are required to deal adequately with these students' needs such as well-trained behavior support teams and school crisis teams.

The core concepts in the model presented in this chapter for correcting the full range of problem behavior are twofold: (a) The system needs to have a continuum of procedures for addressing the full range of problem behavior, and (b) this continuum is broken out into two tracks, office-managed behavior and staff-managed behavior.

Office-managed behavior refers to the response to the behaviors that are very serious and usually relate to school safety, legal issues, and classroom disruption. In this model, it is expected that teachers and staff manage the remaining behaviors themselves, usually in the context where the behaviors occur. Procedures were described for each of these tracks.

Experience has shown that if these procedures (or similar procedures) are consistently followed, office referrals will be reduced, occurrences of expected behavior will be increased, and the overall teaching-learning environment of the school and district will be enhanced.

10

Step 6. Using the Data

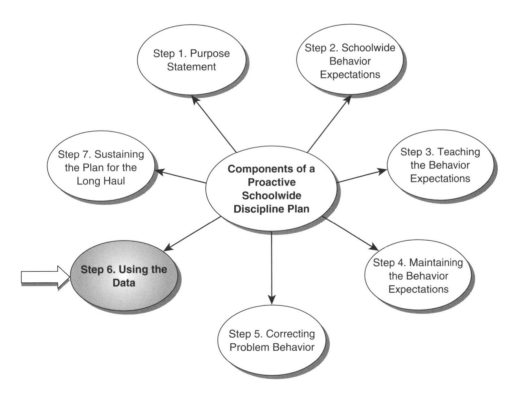

The next section in the steps for developing a proactive approach to schoolwide discipline is the data management system. On the surface, it would appear a quite straightforward step. Essentially, fields need to be developed for the data entry (such as student information, infraction, referring teacher, and action taken). These data are entered into a spreadsheet, and reports can be gleaned in many ways. Moreover, there are several data management system software programs readily available for schools.

However, maintaining the data entries and, more important, using the data for holding accountability, making decisions, and evaluating programs have not been strong points in schools and districts in general. Several authors and researchers have noted the adoption of evidence-based technologies has been limited and short term (Biglan, 1995; Latham, 1988; Sugai & Horner, 2006). Greenberg et al. (2003) pointed out that many schools are not sufficiently coordinated to attend to the factors that maximize the measurable program outcomes. Carnine (2002) pointed out the disconcerting result that the decisions made by educational leaders and experts are mostly based on a whole range of highly questionable reasons excluding scientific research and that their decisions are not accountable in terms of measurable outcomes. He concluded that "until education becomes the kind of profession that reveres evidence, we should not be surprised to find its experts dispensing unproven methods, endlessly flitting from one fad to another" (Carnine, 2002, p. 3).

While the big picture in education regarding the reliable use of evidence-based practices may be quite disconcerting, considerable gains can be made and have been made in effective use of office-referral data in schools. However, strong leadership is definitely needed for effectual and efficient data management systems to be implemented and maintained. This leadership must be provided by the building team, with the school administrator member on the team playing a major role.

In developing a data management system for a proactive schoolwide discipline plan, the following components are crucial: (a) defining the role of the leadership team, (b) knowing the purposes of an effective data management system, and (c) having guidelines in developing a data management system.

◼ DEFINING THE ROLE OF THE LEADERSHIP TEAM

As indicated previously, the leadership team has a critical role in ensuring where data are collected and used in the schoolwide plan. The following suggestions for the team have been gleaned from districts where data collection is in place and is used to guide implementation and maintain the plan.

Determine a Data Management System

There are several options for determining which kind of system should be used in an individual school or district. These options include a self-generated program, a commercial program, or a Web-based program such as the School-Wide Information System (SWIS) plan developed at the University of Oregon (www.swis.org). It does not seem to matter which system is used as long as the data are reliably collected, entered, and used.

Designate a Data Entry Person

Someone on the staff needs to be given the responsibility to enter the data on a regular basis. This person needs to be fully trained and given the time to make the entries. It is also necessary to have a backup person trained and available in case the designated person is on leave for sickness or other reasons. The designated person may or may not be a member of the team. Many schools use the secretary for this purpose.

Monitor Data Entry

Once someone has been designated to enter the data, the next step is to ensure that the data are being entered on the scheduled basis. Typically, the school administrator on the team touches base with the data-entry designee on a weekly basis for the first few weeks. In this way, the administrator can gauge if the data are being entered, and if not, address the issue and problem solve as needed.

Gather Reports Weekly

The team should receive data reports on a weekly or every-other-week schedule. In this way, the team becomes educated in reviewing the data, and trends can be readily seen on a regular basis. It is highly desirable to have one team member responsible for collecting these reports.

Present the Reports to the Faculty

In this model, the team makes ongoing contact with the faculty. The schoolwide discipline plan should be a standard item on the faculty meeting agenda. This time slot should be frequently used to present data findings to the faculty. Summary graphs and reports can also be disseminated through the mail or message box system in the school. The faculty should be notified when these reports are distributed and informed that there will be opportunities for discussion and decision making scheduled at the next faculty meeting.

Use the Data for Decision Making

Most important, the team must provide leadership in how the data are to be used in decision making. For example, the data may indicate that there has been an increase in office referrals at recess or in hallways over the past month. This information is then used to develop a plan to address the reasons for the referrals, and a draft plan is developed. The data and plan are taken to the faculty for discussion and adoption. The ideal would be that over time, if the data suggest a problem, there is the expectation that the team and faculty will address the problem.

Disseminate Results

It is important for the team to disseminate the data results on a regular basis to stakeholders including parents, the district office, board members, and the community as appropriate. This practice will enable progress to be identified and celebrated as appropriate.

■ PURPOSES OF AN EFFECTIVE DATA MANAGEMENT SYSTEM

The key to an effective proactive schoolwide discipline plan is the systematic use of data. The following reasons are presented to highlight the importance for schools and districts to adopt and fully use data management systems.

Tracking Progress

First and foremost, a data management system enables the team and faculty members to answer this fundamental question regarding any plan or innovation: "Is the plan working?" For example, if one school's office referrals were reduced by 25% from one year to the next after implementing a proactive schoolwide discipline plan, it could be concluded that the plan is working because office referrals are decreasing. In Figure 10.1, an illustration is presented depicting the significant reduction in office referrals over a three-year period as a function of implementing a proactive discipline plan.

Figure 10.1   Elementary School Reduction in Office Referrals

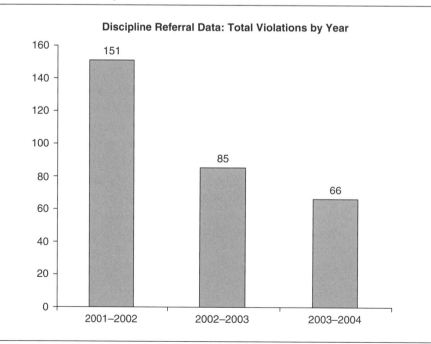

SOURCE: Courtesy of Anchorage School District.

Given that all staff are expected to do their part in implementing the plan, they need assurances that the plan is working. In this case, the reduction in office referrals is strong testimony to acknowledge the efforts of staff and to ensure the efforts will continue.

Basis for Decision Making

There are two levels of decisions that can be made arising from a review of data: (a) overall progress and (b) specific components.

Overall Progress. Once a data management system is in place, the team and faculty are in a position to evaluate the overall progress of the plan. If the data show a significant reduction in office referrals, the decision would be to maintain the plan. However, if there is only a modest change or no change, and maybe an increase in office referrals, the team needs to make different decisions.

The first question always to be asked is, "Is the faculty implementing the plan as intended?" Sometimes, some faculty members may not have started to implement the plan; others may be implementing the plan but changing it to suit their positions. To determine the root cause of the lack of fidelity, the team may need to hold a frank discussion with staff and conduct some observations around the building to see if faculty is following the details of the plan. The outcome might be to identify the roadblocks inhibiting fidelity of implementation and then problem solve. For example, if the faculty is implementing the plan as intended, then a second question is, "What modifications are needed to strengthen the plan?" It may be that supervision needs to be increased, more teaching may be needed on the schoolwide behavior expectations, more positive responses to displays of expected behavior may be needed, or consequences following office referrals may need to be changed. Basically, a faculty decision is made on how to modify the plan, and the results are reviewed in a few weeks time.

Specific Components. As will be discussed later in this chapter, the data can be analyzed or cut in many different ways. For example, the office-referral data can be broken down into referrals by grade, location, time of day, individual students, kind of behavior, referring teacher, ethnicity, and gender. These analyses enable pinpoints to be made as to where the majority of referrals are coming from, and specific plans can be made to address these particular areas. Figure 10.2 presents a graph for one term from a school depicting the break-out of office referrals by behavior.

It is very clear from the graph that the majority of referrals have been for fighting. In this case, the team would examine where the fighting examples are occurring most frequently and develop a specific plan. If, for example, the fighting occurs mostly at recess, the plan might involve the teachers providing more instruction on how to play appropriately at recess, remind the students of the recess expectations (from the schoolwide behavior expectation matrix described in Chapter 6), review supervision, and provide feedback to the students on how they displayed the recess behavior expectations. The data would be reviewed in a few weeks after the particular plan has been implemented to determine if the referrals for fighting at recess have been reduced. Moreover, the other problem behaviors would be monitored, and if problems persist, plans would be developed to address these concerns.

Figure 10.2   Incidents by Behavior

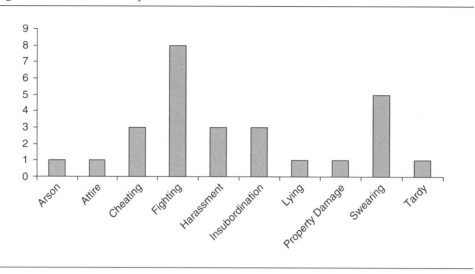

SOURCE: Courtesy of Educational Resource Associates.

Data enable the team to analyze the specific areas of concern and set up a decision to act on the data with a particular plan to address these concerns. Again, a desirable data management system would be designed so that data enable specific problem areas to be identified, with the expectation that a decision would follow to address these concerns with a specific behavior plan.

Data Serving as a Catalyst for Interventions

In some cases, especially if staff are highly motivated to achieve solid results for its students, merely the act of looking at data will prompt action if the data indicate problems. It is just like a person stepping on the scales, being shocked or bothered by the numbers, and then becoming motivated to develop a plan to lose weight.

An elementary school had a pre-office referral step of "time out," which meant that students who displayed unacceptable behavior in class were sent to another classroom or supervised area. Data on the frequency of these time outs were taken, and the results presented to the faculty. The principal indicated that

> I found that the simple act of reviewing the data on a classroom and schoolwide basis (as well as on an individual basis) was an intervention in and of itself. No one even knew the extent of the problem, even though there was a plan. (personal communication)

Once the teachers saw the data, their efforts became more focused in implementing a proactive schoolwide plan. The results presented in Figure 10.3 showed a significant reduction on time outs over the next two years.

Figure 10.3   Reduction in Time Outs Over Two Years

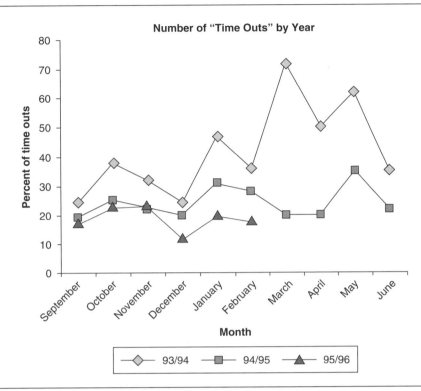

SOURCE: Courtesy of Anchorage School District.

These data also served to provide direct feedback to students who were receiving high rates of time outs. As one of the teachers reported:

> The monthly timeout records help students see the big picture of themselves and improvements they are making over time. They help me help the student pinpoint areas for goal setting. The student(s) and I sit down together and set goals for the following month. This really seems to help the students who struggle with their behavior. (Fifth-grade teacher, personal communication)

Track Behavior Patterns

The data can also be used to track behavior patterns and trends either over time during the year or over several years. Once the patterns are identified, decisions can be made to develop specific plans to address these trends. By collecting the same data over time, the effectiveness of the plan in changing these patterns can be gauged.

The data in Figure 10.4 show the office referrals by month.

It is relatively easy to see an increase in office referrals later in the year. This trend shows a sharp increase in referrals in February, which maintains through May. The referrals drop off in June, which can be explained by June being a much shorter month ending the school year. These data imply that the faculty may need to provide more effort with the school-wide plan and to reach agreements on where in the plan they should provide more focus and consistency.

Figure 10.4   Office Referrals by Month Showing Trends

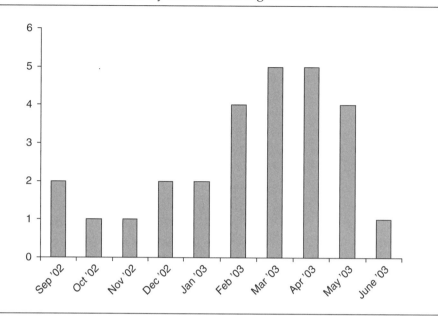

SOURCE: Courtesy of Educational Resource Associates.

Identifying Special-Needs Students With Behavior Issues

As was noted in Chapter 2, Figure 2.1, students identified as having special needs regarding behavior issues represent about 5% of the student body. These students typically do not respond to universal interventions offered by a schoolwide proactive discipline plan. It is very important to identify these students as early as possible so that appropriate, individualized behavior support plans can be developed. Otherwise, if the needs of these students are not addressed, it will not be very long before teachers may conclude that the schoolwide plan is not working, resulting in less effort to implement the plan reliably.

In addition, the break-out by individual students provides important information or documentation that can be addressed at parent meetings. Also, these reports may be needed to document student needs by other agencies that may be involved with the student, such as child abuse agencies and case managers for mental health departments and juvenile crime services.

Figure 10.5, Identifying Students With Multiple Office Referrals, provides an example of breaking out the data from the office-referral database by students who have more than two office-referrals over a period of two terms. Students with the highest number of referrals would subsequently become target students for individual behavior support plans. The remaining students would receive some support, such as counseling or a parent conference.

Figure 10.5   Identifying Students With Multiple Office Referrals

Number of Referrals	15	4	3	10	3	9	3	6	4
Name of Student	Brock	Candy	Elgin	Francine	Lana	Petry	Rachel	Simone	Ian
Student Number	1	2	3	4	5	6	7	8	9

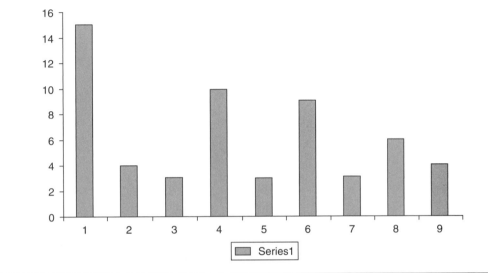

SOURCE: Courtesy of Educational Resource Associates.

Working With Individual Teachers

One of the most difficult aspects of data analysis for decision making is using the data to help individual teachers. In some cases, it is clear that the majority of referrals, especially from classrooms, come from individual teachers. In these cases, the teacher may need additional assistance in addressing the problems. Careful attention must be given to how this information is communicated and addressed with a teacher, otherwise there could be problems with the teacher's union if individual teachers are singled out in this way. It is best to set an expectation before the data system is implemented that one of the ways the data will be analyzed is by individual teachers making the referrals. In addition, it is important that any break-outs on these lines are conducted with all teachers, the results treated as confidential, and they are not placed in the teacher's file or used for teacher evaluation purposes. Moreover, any follow-up should be conducted by the school administrator on the team versus teacher team members.

One particular school used the referral data to compare the number of referrals from each teacher with the average number of referrals from all teachers. The administrator simply showed the teachers the results, assured them of confidentiality, and discussed some options for reducing the number of referrals. Figure 10.6 shows the break-out for an individual teacher compared with the average for the entire staff from one year to the

Figure 10.6 Office Referral Comparison of Teacher A to Average Number of Referrals From Teachers Across All Classrooms, 2004/2005 and 2005/2006

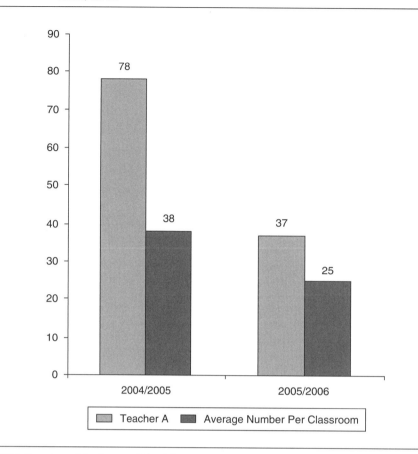

SOURCE: Courtesy of Anchorage School District.

next depicting the significant drop in referrals for the teacher and the reduction in the gap between the referrals by this teacher and the faculty average.

Monitor Disciplinary Actions to Ensure Equity

A major concern across the nation in many areas has been the inequities displayed when data are disaggregated by ethnicity. The proportion of ethnically diverse people in prisons, on death row, in the juvenile system, and living in poverty is significantly higher than the corresponding proportions of the total population. For example, the U.S. Department of Justice (2005) showed that African Americans comprise 13% of the national population, but 41% of incarcerated people. Also, one in three black men between the ages of 20 and 29 was either in jail or prison, or on parole or probation, a rate 3 times higher than for Latino males and 10 times higher than for white males for this age group. The No Child Left Behind Act was essentially spawned by an analysis of academic achievement data by ethnicity (disaggregating the data by race). It was very clear for African American

Figure 10.7   Office Referrals by Ethnicity for First Term

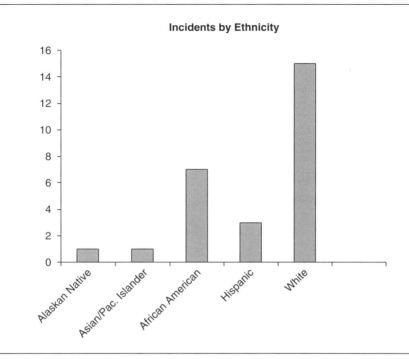

SOURCE: Courtesy of Educational Resource Associates.

students, academic achievement scores were significantly below those of their white counterparts (Togneri & Anderson, 2003).

Similar patterns have been found by disaggregating office-referral data by ethnicity. For example, Figure 10.7 shows the distribution of office referrals by ethnicity over the first term. These data show that African American students received 26% of office referrals, and this group comprises 11% of the school population. In addition, further analysis of the data based on consequences delivered at the office showed that these African American students received 42% of the suspensions delivered.

These data were a powerful eye opener to the faculty and school administrators, resulting in decisions to provide more support for their African American students and to monitor very carefully the suspension responses.

Clearly, it is very important to provide rigorous monitoring of the office-referral data by ethnicity and action taken. These data will quickly draw attention to any inequities and should prompt an appropriate response by the leadership team and faculty.

Goal Setting

It is a common requirement for schools to develop school improvement plans. The impetus for this requirement typically comes from the school board and district office. These plans can show considerable variation, from being very broad, such as to improve the school climate, to concrete measurable outcomes, such as to raise the achievement scores in reading by 20%.

Figure 10.8   Office Referrals for Fighting, Threats, and Violence

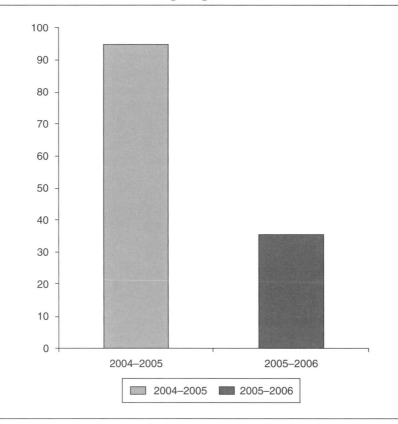

SOURCE: Courtesy of Anchorage School District.

One dimension for school improvement lies in effective use of office-referral data. For example, the school may wish to reduce the inequities of the number of office referrals and suspension action based on ethnicity. Another school may wish to reduce office referrals from classrooms by 25% through providing ongoing professional development on classroom management.

One school decided to set a goal for the year to reduce its office referrals for fighting by 10%. They adopted a specific intervention plan for recess to address fighting and to develop prosocial behaviors on a schoolwide basis using a proactive teaching plan. The results displayed in Figure 10.8 show that their goal of a 10% reduction was not only achieved but exceeded: They had a 60% reduction in office referrals.

Once the faculty, through the leadership provided by the team, become fluent consumers of office-referral data and make decisions based on these data, it is a relatively easy step for them to develop effective school improvement plans. Specifically, the data provide the measuring system to determine if the goal has been met, and the schoolwide proactive discipline plan provides the tools to accomplish the goal. When a school or district achieves or exceeds its goals, as in the previous example, the results should be disseminated and celebrated in some way.

Figure 10.9 Comparison of Third-Grade Reading Proficiency to Schoolwide
Out-of-School Suspensions (Yearly)

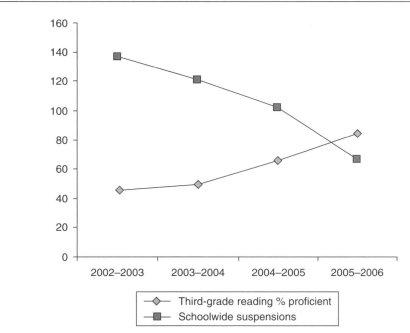

SOURCE: Courtesy of Anchorage School District.

Setting the Stage for Instruction

The primary purpose of the proactive schoolwide discipline plan is to create a positive, safe, supportive, and welcoming environment for all students and staff. Once this environment is established, teachers and educators are in a stronger position to provide instruction. Consequently, it is quite common to see covariation between schoolwide data and academic performance. Logically, we might expect that as the behavior comes more under control, teachers are in a better position to deliver instruction. That is, as the behavior issues decrease, academic achievement should increase. A school in Anchorage, Alaska, found that over a three-year period, the number of suspensions progressively decreased and the reading scores progressively increased (see Figure 10.9).

These results must be particularly gratifying to the school because they are keeping more students in school by reducing suspensions and, at the same time, increasing their reading scores. It is important to note there is no claim that significant changes in behavioral data will directly cause academic results to increase. For academic results to increase, careful attention needs to be paid to instructional interventions such as adopting effective curricula, using sound instructional practices, and following assessment procedures. However, the claim is made that when an effective schoolwide discipline plan is in place, the stage is set for providing quality instruction and that the converse is also true, in that when a school has serious schoolwide behavioral issues, quality instruction becomes more difficult to implement.

■ GUIDELINES IN DEVELOPING A DATA MANAGEMENT SYSTEM

It is very clear that an office-referral data system is a powerful tool that greatly assists the implementation and maintenance of a proactive school-wide discipline system. However, several issues need to be addressed to ensure that the data system is efficient. If the system becomes cumbersome, it will be used less and less, and the whole process will begin to falter. The following guidelines are designed to ensure that the system is manageable and friendly.

Ease of Data Entry

The system needs to be set up so the data entry person can input the information with relative ease. The office-referral form is the key. This form needs to be simple and designed in a checklist format so the items can be readily entered into the data system. The system must be integrated with the school's discipline plan and office-referral procedures.

Keeping Current

The data entry must be up to date so that current reports can be readily accessible. In some cases, the forms are not turned in in a timely manner or completed correctly. The team must monitor each of these concerns to make sure the forms are turned in as early as reasonable and completed correctly. The management of the data system should become an integral and highly valued part of the school and district operations.

Developing a Confidentiality Protocol

The school and district must develop a strict confidentiality protocol and ensure that it is followed by faculty. Typically, students are assigned numbers for data entry, and certain faculty are designated to access the data.

Ease of Generating Reports

The team and the faculty need to see data reports on a regular basis. The ideal would be that reviewing the data would become a standard agenda item for every team and faculty meeting. To accomplish this level of use, the data system must be designed so that a full range of reports can be generated. These reports need to be available in simple statistical formats, such as tables listing the number of referrals for fighting over a four-week period. The reports can also be presented in graphical formats (usually column graphs or pie charts), which enable trends to be examined visually. In addition, summary reports need to be accessible on relatively short notice. For example, an emergency meeting may be called for a special-needs student. It is very helpful to have a report of this student's behavior over a recent period available for the meeting. Finally, the data system needs to have the capacity to generate a variety of break-outs or disaggregations. For example, data trends over a two-year period may be needed or a break-out of referral data by month, grade level, location, or class of behavior.

Data reports are the key to using data and making decisions. These reports need to be generated on a frequent basis involving a variety of report formats, and the process needs to be relatively easy.

Getting Started

The very first consideration in getting started with developing and implementing a data management system is to determine which system to use. The common available systems include self-generated programs, districtwide systems, commercial programs, and Web-based systems.

An essential step, regardless of the system used, is that the office-referral form must be congruent with the data system. Information collected on the office-referral form must be directly entered into the database. This implies, as noted earlier in this chapter, that care must be taken in developing an office-referral form to identify and include the major fields, such as student information, kind of infraction, location, referring staff member, and action taken. The remaining steps that facilitate tracking and report writing are tied to the various links that are created or available in the computer-based program.

SUMMARY ■

The data management system is the key to maintaining a proactive school-wide management system. This system, if used on a regular basis, provides the necessary information for making critical decisions about the schoolwide plan. The data system allows a fundamental question to be answered: "Is the proactive schoolwide discipline plan working?" If the answer is yes, decisions are made to maintain the plan. If the answer is no or "no to some extent," decisions are made to modify the plan based on the pinpoints that can be made through the data analysis. In effect, the data management system permits the plan to be evaluated and accountability to be operative.

Unfortunately, data management and decision making based on data are not universally standard procedures in schools. For the data management system to be effective, the leadership team must play a highly active role in reviewing the data on a regular basis. In addition, the team must bring data reports to the faculty, preferably at every faculty meeting. The ideal is that data management and decision making based on the data become standard routines in schools and districts.

11

Step 7. Sustaining the Plan for the Long Haul

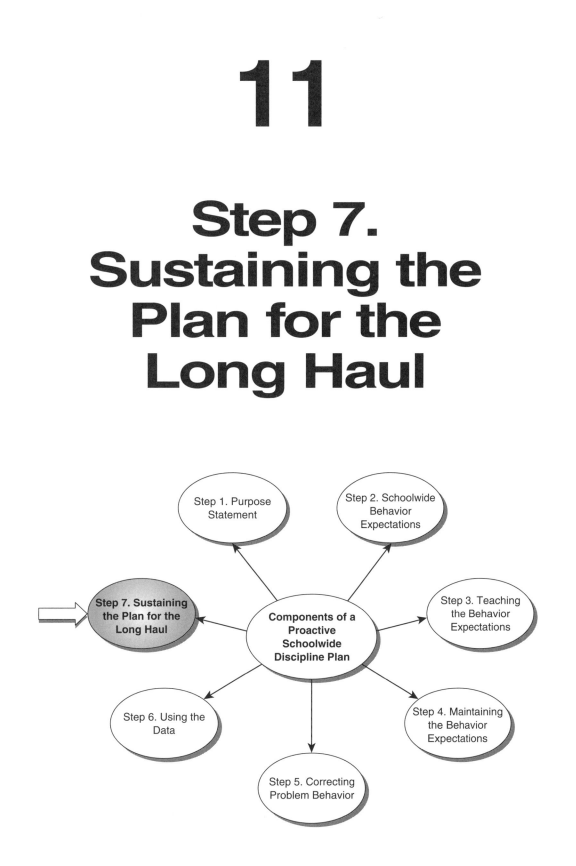

At this juncture, the first six components have been described. The typical practice for schools is to implement these components one at a time over a full school year. In most cases, results are very encouraging, and the faculty is strongly behind the plan. However, even though the plan may show initial success, systematic steps need to be taken over the following years to ensure the plan is sustained. If such steps are not taken, there is, unfortunately, a high likelihood that the plan may slowly become diluted or even abandoned. Research has shown over several decades that many effective and promising programs in public schools are often fully adopted initially only to be systematically weakened or discarded over time (Baker, Gersten, Dimino, & Griffiths, 2004; Grimes & Tilly, 1996; Latham, 1988; Slavin, 1989; Sugai & Horner, 2006). These researchers have noted several reasons for the failure of schools to sustain programs, such as a change in leadership especially the principal, budget changes, a shift in priorities at school or district level, competing initiatives mandated by district or state offices, burnout for leadership team members, fidelity drift in following the procedures, and lack of response to data.

The purpose of this final component is to provide steps designed to ensure that the proactive schoolwide discipline plan presented in this book is sustained. The strategies fall into two categories: (a) ongoing refresh training for the leadership team, and (b) systemic-based steps to ensure sustainability.

■ ONGOING REFRESH MEETINGS FOR THE LEADERSHIP TEAM

When a school elects to implement a proactive schoolwide plan, there is usually an entire day devoted to providing the leadership team with in-service training on the whole model. This training typically is conducted at the end of the preceding year, just prior to the commencement of the new school year, or very early in the targeted school year. The training is normally conducted by a specialist in this area, or the team uses material from other sources, such as the material presented in this book. In most cases, it takes a full year to implement the first six components.

In the second year, and ideally in each of the following years, the leadership team should spend at least a half day reviewing the status of the plan and developing action responses as needed. These review sessions have been called "leadership team refresh meetings." The basic approach for these sessions is to take each component of the proactive schoolwide plan and respond to a set of questions to assess the respective levels of implementation. Consensus in the team is determined for the responses to these questions, and action plans are developed based on the results. If the team is satisfied with the level of implementation, the decision is to maintain the component as is. If there are concerns regarding any component, an action plan is developed to address the problems. A comprehensive checklist and action plan is presented in Appendix Q: Form 11.1, Checklist and Action Plan for Leadership Team Refresh Meetings, located in the Appendices section. Box 11.1 presents an example of the results and action plans for the Gilbert High School building leadership team meeting at the close of the school year.

BOX 11.1	An Example of a Checklist and Action Plan for Gilbert High School's Leadership Team Refresh Meeting		

Component of Proactive Schoolwide Plan	In Place	
Building Leadership Team	Yes	No
1. Do we have one?		
2. Is it representative of our staff (administration, general-education teachers, special-education teachers, specialist teachers, support staff, classified staff)?	Yes	No
3. Are team meetings frequent enough?	Yes	No
4. Does the team present and share information with faculty on a sufficiently regular basis?	Yes	No
Action Response: Building Leadership Team		
Hold meetings every other week at 8:00 A.M. on Wednesdays.		
Component 1: Purpose Statement		
1. Do we have a purpose statement?	Yes	No
2. Was it developed with opportunity for staff input?	Yes	No
3. Is the purpose statement printed in the staff/student manual?	Yes	No
4. Has the purpose statement been communicated to students?	Yes	No
5. Has the purpose statement been communicated to parents?	Yes	No
6. Does the purpose statement have learning outcomes specified?	Yes	No
Action Response: Purpose Statement		
During the first week of school when students return, all homeroom teachers remind the students of the purpose statement and include a paragraph in the first Gilbert News *to be sent to the parents.*		
Component 2: Schoolwide Behavior Expectations		
1. Are the schoolwide behaviors identified?	Yes	No
2. Did all staff have the opportunity to provide input?	Yes	No
3. Are the behaviors posted?	Yes	No
Schoolwide Behavior Matrix		
4. Are all the major school settings targeted?	Yes	No
5. Are the specific behaviors identified for each setting in the matrix?	Yes	No
6. Is the matrix posted?	Yes	No
Action Response: Schoolwide Behavior Expectations		
We should change posters throughout the year to catch students' attention. Get help from the art department.		
Component 3: Teaching the Behavior Expectations		
1. Were the behaviors taught in all classes?	Yes	No
2. Do students receive frequent reminders of the behaviors (such as in class, during announcements)?	Yes	No
3. Are the specific behaviors in each setting of the matrix taught?	Yes	No
4. Are reminders provided for the specific behaviors in each setting in the matrix?	Yes	No
Action Response: Teaching Schoolwide Behavior Expectations		
All homeroom teachers will be asked to provide reminders to their students on the settings listed in the matrix. We will have a schedule and target one setting per month.		

(Continued)

BOX 11.1 (Continued)		
Component of Proactive Schoolwide Plan	In Place	
Component 4: Maintaining the Schoolwide Behavior Expectations		
1. Do schoolwide events occur to recognize students for exhibiting expected behaviors?	Yes	No
2. Are staff clear on procedures for these events or awards?	Yes	No
3. Is staff participation in the process adequate?	Yes	No
4. Do students value the events or awards?	Yes	No
5. Are the recognition awards publicized sufficiently?	Yes	No
Action Response: Maintaining the Behavior Expectations		
Greater effort needs to be made to involve all staff in the process. More reminders will be given, and informal contacts made to ensure greater participation by the faculty.		
Component 5: Correcting Problem Behavior		
1. Have staff developed criteria for which behaviors warrant office referrals and which should be managed by staff?	Yes	No
2. Does the office-referral form reflect those behaviors warranting referrals?	Yes	No
3. Does the office-referral form include reasons for referral, description of problem, and action taken?	Yes	No
4. Do teachers have support structures for managing staff-managed problem behavior (behavior not warranting an office referral)?	Yes	No
5. Does the administration have options for responding to the full range of office-referral behavior?	Yes	No
6. Are behavior support teams operative for responding to chronic problem behavior?	Yes	No
7. Are crisis teams in place to deal with emergency behavior?	Yes	No
Action Response: Correcting Problem Behavior		
Arrange faculty meeting time to provide more inservice training on how teachers can work together more for addressing staff-managed behavior. Also provide inservice opportunities for the behavior support team. Suspension rates are still relatively high, so we need to look more into alternatives to suspension this coming year.		
Component 6: Using the Data		
1. Does a leadership team member serve as data coordinator?	Yes	No
2. Has the data coordinator received sufficient training to oversee data management system?	Yes	No
3. Is a system in place for entering office-referral data on a regular basis?	Yes	No
4. Is an individual person assigned the task of entering data?	Yes	No
5. Does the data entry match the office-referral form?	Yes	No
6. Are data presented and reviewed by leadership team and staff on a regular basis?	Yes	No
7. Are data used for making decisions?	Yes	No
8. Are data disseminated to all stakeholders?	Yes	No
Action Response: Using the Data		
Generally, we are pleased with the data system. It is the first time we have anything systematic. However, we need to get the district technology people in to help the coordinator with some questions. Also, we need to sharpen the focus on the data analysis so decisions can be made, especially in areas to target. Finally, we need to get summaries of the data to parents and district office more frequently—at least once a semester.		

If a number of the components of the schoolwide plan need an action plan, the leadership team needs to prioritize the action responses and develop a schedule to implement each action plan.

Note: These refresh meetings also serve as an inservice opportunity for new members on the leadership team.

SYSTEMIC-BASED STEPS TO ENSURE SUSTAINABILITY

Until now, this book has centered on describing steps for developing a proactive schoolwide discipline plan. However, when the total operation of the school is considered, it is obvious that this plan is just one aspect of the many activities conducted in schools. Consequently, if the schoolwide discipline plan takes into account how the plan fits in with other programs and plans within the school, innovations and new programs that are subsequently introduced must be seen to fit in with the schoolwide plan and other existing programs. In other words, for plans to be sustained in a school, a systems approach should be used.

The basis of this model is that all aspects of school improvement must be systematically addressed on an ongoing basis. The purpose of this section is to present a summary of key details to be responded to by the leadership team each year following initial implementation (Colvin, Braun, Cole, Paine, & Tobin, 2006). It is this yearly review and action response that will ensure the proactive schoolwide plan will be sustained. These key points are briefly described followed by a checklist and response plan.

Key Systemic Factors for Sustaining the Schoolwide Discipline Plan and Process

Ongoing Data Reports. A data management system should be firmly in place and reports generated on a regular basis. These reports should permit comparisons to be made on aspects of office-referral data year by year. These comparisons should set the stage for decisions to be made on whether to sustain the plan without change, modify the plan, or make substantial changes depending on the data trends.

Administrative Support. The entire school and district administration must commit to the program both initially and long term. This includes support from the district office, including the school board, superintendent, assistant superintendent, and supervisors (such as the special-education director or curriculum director) and school principals.

Faculty Support. Typically, the faculty is expected to implement and maintain the program; therefore, it is crucial to take the necessary steps to fully inform them of the details of the program and progress on an ongoing basis.

Allocation of Resources for the Long Term. The school or district must make a long-term financial commitment to the program for it to be sustained. The resources must be written into the budget like any other long-term item such as transportation and food services. Moreover, if the adopted plan involves expansion in the future, these costs must be predetermined and written into the budget for that time.

Comprehensive Professional Development. All personnel who have responsibilities for program implementation must be given the necessary professional development. Professional development needs to be ongoing. New administrators and new faculty will most likely need specific induction and training.

Ongoing Data System. A data system must be in place before implementation occurs. This data management system permits progress to be determined for both the short term and long term. Data must be reviewed on a regular basis. The leadership team should generate summary reports of the data to determine progress and whether the plan is meeting the goals of the purpose statement.

Wall-to-Wall Planning. Wall-to-wall planning targets every aspect of the operation versus isolated parts. The planning is designed to cover all the bases and to anticipate the impact of the program on all key areas such as staff involvement, student outcomes, and short- and long-term planning. The plan must be adapted as necessary to be consistent with the school and district culture and with existing innovations, plans, and structures.

Logistical Details Maintained. The many "nuts-and-bolts" details necessary for starting the plan need to be maintained. These include getting supplies, making contacts, appointing staff members to take charge of certain activities, scheduling meeting times and places, and scheduling support activities. This planning needs to occur during the first week of the new school year.

Fidelity of Implementation. One of the biggest problems with sustaining programs is called "fidelity drift." The program may begin with everyone implementing it as planned, but as time goes on, some staff members may revert to other methods and lose the integrity of the initial plan. The leadership team, with the administrator playing a key role, must develop a monitoring plan to ensure that staff members are implementing the program properly both initially and over time.

Problem-Solving Plan. Problems often arise with initial implementation. Structures need to be in place so that these problems can be addressed in a timely manner. A building-based leadership team is a common structure used in the schools to assist with implementation and, in particular, to address problems and develop workable solutions.

Communication of Progress. Progress reports should be made available to all stakeholders. The leadership team should generate summary reports to be presented and discussed at faculty meetings on a regular basis. Recognition should occur to mark successes and to acknowledge the effort of the faculty.

Integration With Existing Programs. New initiatives or plans should not be introduced without addressing their potential impact on existing programs. The ideal is to show how these new programs can be integrated with current innovations and thereby lessen the chance of the current effective programs being compromised or discontinued.

BOX 11.2   Example of the Results and Action Plans From Gilbert High School's Leadership Team for Sustaining the Schoolwide Plan

Systemic Factor	Response	
1. Have ongoing data reports been conducted?	~~Yes~~	No
2. Has administrative support been established and continued?	~~Yes~~	No
3. Has faculty support been established and continued?	~~Yes~~	No
4. Has allocation of resources occurred?	~~Yes~~	No
5. Has comprehensive professional development been planned?	Yes	~~No~~
6. Has an ongoing data system been developed?	Yes	~~No~~
7. Is the data system operating?	~~Yes~~	No
8. Are decisions based on data?	Yes	~~No~~
9. Has wall-to-wall planning occurred?	~~Yes~~	No
10. Have major logistical details been planned?	~~Yes~~	No
11. Is fidelity of implementation being monitored?	Yes	~~No~~
12. Is there a problem-solving plan?	~~Yes~~	No
13. Is progress information being communicated?	Yes	~~No~~
14. Is the new program integrated with existing programs?	~~Yes~~	No
15. Is staff continuity considered with new hires?	~~Yes~~	No
16. Are involved staff members supported?	~~Yes~~	No

Action Responses

The team concluded that several of these items were beyond their responsibility. Bob (principal) said he would raise the issues at the next cabinet meeting at the district office.

We need to organize summary data so we can see at a glance semester-by-semester and year-by-year data patterns. Summary data need to be made available to parents and the district office at least once a semester. Bob (principal) said he would follow up with all faculty that they are expected to implement the plan, and he will make periodic checks to see that plan is implemented faithfully.

SOURCE: Adapted with permission from Colvin, Braun, Cole, Paine, and Tobin (2006).

Staff Continuity. There are always turnovers with administration and staff. New hires should be carefully screened regarding their experience and commitment to existing successful programs. In this way, programs will not be compromised because new staff have other priorities or their own agendas. Professional development should be available for new hires as needed to ensure they are competent to maintain the plan.

Supporting Involved Staff. Quite often, staff members receive a lot of recognition in the early phases of program implementation for their work and success. However, as time goes on this, recognition often recedes. Staff members need ongoing support and recognition.

A comprehensive checklist and action plan is presented in Appendix R: Form 11.2, Checklist and Action Response for Sustaining the Schoolwide Plan, located in the Appendices section. The checklist and action response should be completed once a year, either at the end of the school year or as early as possible in the new school year. Box 11.2 presents an example of the results and action plans for Gilbert High School's leadership team for sustaining their schoolwide plan.

■ SUMMARY

While this chapter may be the last component described for developing a proactive schoolwide discipline plan, it may well be the most important one. The reason is that it addresses how to sustain the plan. Unfortunately, many schools and districts have a long history of implementing programs that begin with a flurry of energy from the faculty and district office and, in many cases, enjoy very positive results. However, as time goes on, these programs often give way to other innovations, become significantly weakened, and often disappear.

For a plan to be maintained, specific procedures must be in place to sustain the plan. Excellent results have been obtained in this area of sustainability by using two broad strategies: (a) conducting refresh sessions with the building leadership team each year, in which the various components of the plan are checked for adequate implementation and action plans are developed accordingly, and (b) working with the operating factors inherent in school systems.

Concluding Remarks

There is no question that schools are under considerable pressure to expand their capacity to meet a whole array of student needs. While these needs are very legitimate, it becomes a formidable task for schools and districts to meet them. The purpose of this book is to provide clear, well-documented steps for developing a proactive schoolwide discipline plan. There is a very simple assumption that if the students are reasonably well behaved and the school environment is essentially positive, then educators will have more chance to maximize their teaching. By contrast, if discipline problems abound, teachers and administrators will spend a great deal of time and energy in addressing these issues, resulting in less teaching time.

The steps presented in this book have been implemented successfully in many schools and school districts around America and Canada with substantial documentation. However, there is no "silver bullet" in the model. The tasks take considerable effort and commitment from faculty, administration, and leaders from the district office. Moreover, implementation is not a "one-shot thing" in which, once the plan is under way, it will maintain itself. Rather, the plan, once implemented, will need ongoing effort and commitment to be sustained.

While this plan can ensure a safe and welcoming environment for students, there is no assumption that *all* students will behave appropriately. Some students will need more behavioral support than what is presented in this book. These students may need individual plans within the school and, in some cases, support beyond the school setting. However, it is argued that having a solid schoolwide plan will give the individual plans for more challenging students a greater chance of succeeding.

Moreover, there is no assumption that the proactive discipline plan will, of itself, cause students to learn more. The assumption is that students and teachers will have an environment that is more conducive to teaching and learning. Turnbull et al. (2002) expressed very aptly the need to "establish responsive environments that 'stack the deck' in favor of appropriate student behavior and quality of life outcomes" (p. 1). This book is about "stacking the deck" so that educators have the tools they need for their students to be safe and successful.

Appendices

NOTE: These appendices may be reproduced or adapted for personal use in the classroom, school, or district.

Appendix A

Form 4.1   Checklist for Determining the Adequacy of an Existing Schoolwide Discipline Plan

YES	NO	1.	The purpose of schoolwide discipline is clearly stated.
YES	NO	2.	Schoolwide behavior expectations are clearly stated.
YES	NO	3.	Schoolwide procedures are in place to teach expected behaviors.
YES	NO	4.	Schoolwide practices are in place to recognize demonstrations of expected behavior.
YES	NO	5.	Staff members are clear as to which behavior should be dealt with by staff and which should warrant office referrals.
YES	NO	6.	Procedures are in place for staff to work together to address persistent, minor behavior.
YES	NO	7.	A continuum of steps is available to address serious office-referral–level behavior.
YES	NO	8.	Procedures are in place to use building resources to assist students who display chronic, serious behavior.
YES	NO	9.	Procedures are in place to address crises or emergencies.
YES	NO	10.	Data-keeping procedures are in place to track student behavior.
YES	NO	11.	Data are used to make planning decisions.
YES	NO	12.	Procedures are in place to sustain the plan.

_____   Number of YES responses

_____   Number of NO responses

MARK DECISION

_____ *More than eight YES responses:* Maintain existing program and develop plan to address inadequacies, if necessary.

_____ *Fewer than eight YES responses:* Establish and develop a building leadership team to assist staff in developing a proactive schoolwide discipline plan.

Appendix B

Form 4.2   Worksheet for a Leadership Team

Name of School _____

Name	Title	E-mail	Telephone (Extension or Cell)
Group E-mail			

Team Meetings

Frequency _____   Location _____

Time   _____   Day   _____

Faculty Meetings

Frequency _____   Location _____

Time   _____   Day   _____

Allocated Time _____

Next Meeting Date _____

Decision Process and Criterion

Procedure _____

Criterion _____

Appendix C

Form 4.3   Building Team Minutes

School _____   Date _____

Present _____   _____

_____   _____

_____   _____

_____   _____

Time _____ to _____   Location _____

Updates

    New Discussion/Activities

    Decisions

    Items to Present to Faculty

    Items:

    Team Member(s) Presenting Items:

    Other

    Next Meeting:

    Next Chair:

Appendix D

Form 4.4 Checklist for Building Leadership Team-Based Process

Process Factor	In Place	
1. Establishing the Need for a Plan		
1.1 Schoolwide discipline plan survey conducted and scored	Yes	No
1.2 Results discussed at school or building level	Yes	No
1.3 Overview of plan (components and evidence base) presented to faculty or faculties	Yes	No
1.4 Stakeholders informed of plan:		
• School board	Yes	No
• District office	Yes	No
• Building administrators	Yes	No
• Faculties (see Item 2 below)	Yes	No
• Parents	Yes	No
• Students	Yes	No
1.5 Plan is integrated with existing school improvement plans as appropriate	Yes	No
2. Securing Initial Commitment of Faculty		
2.1 Faculty informed of results of needs assessment	Yes	No
2.2 Faculty presented with an overview of proactive schoolwide plan including data from other schools	Yes	No
2.3 Faculty presented with information relating the needs assessment and the plan	Yes	No
2.4 Faculty given opportunity to discuss merits and issues related to plan adoption	Yes	No
2.5 Criterion set for adoption of plan	Yes	No
2.6 Faculty has formal vote on adopting plan	Yes	No
2.7 Preliminary steps reviewed	Yes	No
2.8 Start date determined	Yes	No
2.9 Support expressed by other stakeholders	Yes	No
• School board		
• Superintendent		
• District personnel as appropriate		
• Parent bodies as appropriate		
• Student body as appropriate		
3. Forming a Building Leadership Team		
3.1 Role and responsibilities identified	Yes	No
3.2 Representative groups within faculty identified	Yes	No
3.3 Team selection process determined	Yes	No

Form 4.4 (Continued)

Process Factor	In Place	
3.4 Team selected	Yes	No
3.5 Team is representative of faculty groups	Yes	No
3.6 Faculty notified of team composition	Yes	No
3.7 Student representatives selected	Yes	No
3.8 Parent representatives selected	Yes	No
4. Establishing Roles and Responsibilities		
4.1 Principal	Yes	No
4.2 Team	Yes	No
4.3 Faculty	Yes	No
4.4 School board	Yes	No
4.5 Superintendent	Yes	No
4.6 District office	Yes	No
4.7 Parent body	Yes	No
4.8 Student	Yes	No
5. Developing a Communication System		
5.1 Team meeting scheduled (times and places)	Yes	No
5.2 Team note-taking process and within-team dissemination process determined	Yes	No
5.3 Process for team connecting with faculty determined	Yes	No
5.4 Dissemination process determined for outcomes to be shared with stakeholders	Yes	No
5.5 Structures developed to enable input from faculty and stakeholders	Yes	No
6. Developing an Ongoing Decision-Making Process		
6.1 Data review system developed for team	Yes	No
6.2 Data review system for faculty developed	Yes	No
6.3 Decision-making process developed for team	Yes	No
6.4 Decision-making process developed for faculty	Yes	No

Appendix E

Form 5.1   Worksheet for Developing a Purpose Statement

Directions:

Make a list of the ideas you would like to see included in your Purpose Statement.

The purposes of the schoolwide discipline plan at _____
school is to:

1. _____

   _____

   _____

   _____

2. _____

   _____

   _____

   _____

3. _____

   _____

   _____

   _____

4. _____

   _____

   _____

   _____

Appendix F

Form 5.2   Purpose Statement in Narrative Style

Directions:

Use the points in Form 5.1 to generate a purpose statement in narrative style.

The purpose of the schoolwide discipline plan at _____ school
is to:

_____

_____

_____

_____

_____

_____

_____

_____

_____

Appendix G

Form 5.3   Purpose Statement in Point Style

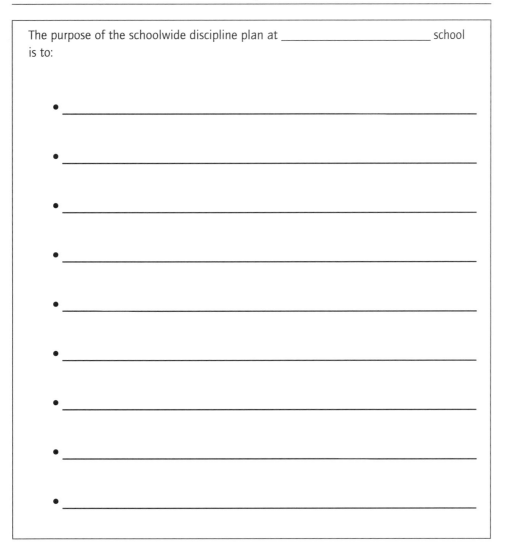

The purpose of the schoolwide discipline plan at _____ school is to:

- _____

- _____

- _____

- _____

- _____

- _____

- _____

- _____

- _____

Appendix H

Form 6.1   Worksheet for Schoolwide Expectations

Schoolwide Behavior Expectations

All students and staff at _____ school
are expected to:

1. _____

    _____

    _____

2. _____

    _____

    _____

3. _____

    _____

    _____

4. _____

    _____

    _____

5. _____

    _____

    _____

Appendix I

Form 6.2   List of Major Common Settings in the School

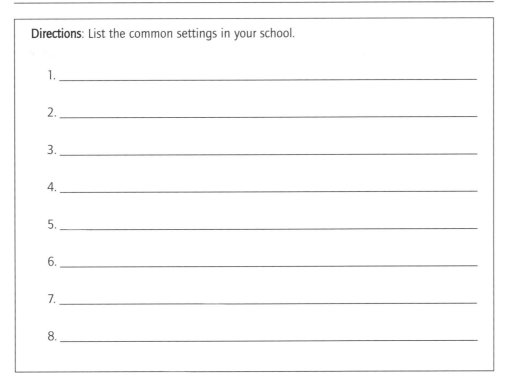

Directions: List the common settings in your school.

1. _____

2. _____

3. _____

4. _____

5. _____

6. _____

7. _____

8. _____

Appendix J

Form 6.3   Common Settings Behavioral Expectations Matrix

Schoolwide Expectations	Common Settings						
1.							
2.							
3.							
4.							
5.							

Appendix K

Form 7.1   Instruction Plan for Teaching a Schoolwide Expectation

Common Setting:

Step 1: Explain
Step 2: Specify student behaviors
Step 3: Practice
Step 4: Monitor
Step 5: Review

Appendix L

Form 7.2   Teaching Behavior Expectations to Older Students and a Maintenance Plan for Younger Students

Schoolwide Behavior Expectation:

Common Setting:

Specific Behaviors:

Remind:

Supervise:

Provide Feedback:

Appendix M

Form 8.1 Schoolwide Recognition Matrix

Award Title	Coordinator	Criteria	Award	Frequency	Presentation	Dissemination

Appendix N

Form 9.1   Worksheet for Office-Referral Behaviors

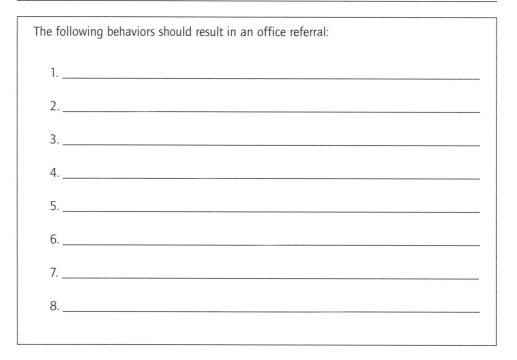

The following behaviors should result in an office referral:

1. _____

2. _____

3. _____

4. _____

5. _____

6. _____

7. _____

8. _____

Appendix O

Form 9.2 Worksheet for Office-Referral Behavior Definitions

Problem Behavior	Definition

Appendix P

Form 9.3   Teacher Team Meeting for Staff-Managed Behavior

☐ Behavior Problem	☐ Academic Problem

Student Name: _____ Grade: _____ Date: _____

Teacher(s): _____ # of Previous Behavior Reports/Staff Meeting: _____

Staff Present: _____

_____

Problem Behavior(s) (2 minutes)	*Expected Behavior(s)* (2 minutes)

Strategies to Teach Expected Behaviors. Select 1–3 (3 minutes)

☐ Reminders	☐ Practice	☐ Parent contact
☐ Reinforcers	☐ Individual contacts	☐ Counseling
☐ Feedback	☐ Monitoring sheet	☐ Tutoring
☐ Contract	☐ Self-management	☐ Modified assignments
☐ Other _____		

Strategies to Correct Problem Behavior(s) (1 minute)

☐ Time out	☐ Parent contact
☐ Loss of privilege	☐ Detention
☐ Other	

Action Plan (5 minutes)

Who	*What*	*When*
_____	_____	_____
_____	_____	_____
_____	_____	_____

Tracking System: _____

_____

Student Conference Date: _____ *Start Date:* _____ *Review Date:* _____

Copies to:

Office File

Teacher

Other: _____

Appendix Q

Form 11.1   Checklist and Action Plan for Leadership Team Refresh Meetings

Component of Proactive Schoolwide Plan	In Place	
Building Leadership Team		
1. Do we have one?	Yes	No
2. Is it representative of our staff (administration, general-education teachers, special-education teachers, specialist teachers, support staff, classified staff)?	Yes	No
3. Are team meetings frequent enough?	Yes	No
4. Does the team present and share information with faculty on a sufficiently regular basis?	Yes	No
Action Response: Building Leadership Team		
Component 1: Purpose Statement		
1. Do we have a purpose statement?	Yes	No
2. Was it developed with opportunity for staff input?	Yes	No
3. Is the purpose statement printed in the staff/student manual?	Yes	No
4. Has the purpose statement been communicated to students?	Yes	No
5. Has the purpose statement been communicated to parents?	Yes	No
6. Does the purpose statement have learning outcomes specified?	Yes	No
Action Response: Purpose Statement		
Component 2: Schoolwide Behavior Expectations		
1. Are the schoolwide behaviors identified?	Yes	No
2. Did all staff have the opportunity to provide input?	Yes	No
3. Are the behaviors posted?	Yes	No
Schoolwide Behavior Matrix		
4. Are all the major school settings targeted?	Yes	No
5. Are the specific behaviors identified for each setting in the matrix?	Yes	No
6. Is the matrix posted?	Yes	No
Action Response: Schoolwide Behavior Expectations		
Component 3: Teaching the Behavior Expectations		
1. Were the behaviors taught in all classes?	Yes	No
2. Do students receive frequent reminders of the behaviors (such as in class, during announcements)?	Yes	No
3. Are the specific behaviors in each setting of the matrix taught?	Yes	No
4. Are reminders provided for the specific behaviors in each setting in the matrix?	Yes	No
Action Response: Teaching the Behavior Expectations		

(Continued)

Appendix Q

Form 11.1 (Continued)

Component of Proactive Schoolwide Plan	In Place	
Component 4: Maintaining the Schoolwide Behavior Expectations		
1. Do schoolwide events occur to recognize students for exhibiting expected behaviors?	Yes	No
2. Are staff clear on procedures for these events or awards?	Yes	No
3. Is staff participation in the process adequate?	Yes	No
4. Do students value the events or awards?	Yes	No
5. Are the recognition awards publicized sufficiently?	Yes	No
Action Response: Maintaining the Behavior Expectations		
Component 5: Correcting Problem Behavior		
1. Have staff developed criteria for which behaviors warrant office referrals and which should be managed by staff?	Yes	No
2. Does the office-referral form reflect those behaviors warranting referrals?	Yes	No
3. Does the office-referral form include reasons for referral, description of problem, and action taken?	Yes	No
4. Do teachers have support structures for managing staff-managed problem behavior (behavior not warranting an office referral)?	Yes	No
5. Does the administration have options for responding to the full range of office-referral behavior?	Yes	No
6. Are behavior support teams operative for responding to chronic problem behavior?	Yes	No
7. Are crisis teams in place to deal with emergency behavior?	Yes	No
Action Response: Correcting Problem Behavior		
Component 6: Using the Data		
1. Does a leadership team member serve as data coordinator?	Yes	No
2. Has the data coordinator received sufficient training to oversee the data management system?	Yes	No
3. Is a system in place for entering office-referral data on a regular basis?	Yes	No
4. Is an individual person assigned the task of entering data?	Yes	No
5. Does the data entry match the office-referral form?	Yes	No
6. Are data presented and reviewed by leadership team and staff on a regular basis?	Yes	No
7. Are data used for making decisions?	Yes	No
8. Are data disseminated to all stakeholders?	Yes	No
Action Response: Developing an Effective Data Management System		

Appendix R

Form 11.2   Checklist and Action Response for Sustaining the Schoolwide Plan

Systemic Factor	Response	
1. Have ongoing data reports been conducted?	Yes	No
2. Has administrative support been established and continued?	Yes	No
3. Has faculty support been established and continued?	Yes	No
4. Has allocation of resources occurred?	Yes	No
5. Has comprehensive professional development been planned?	Yes	No
6. Has an ongoing data system been developed?	Yes	No
7. Is the data system operating?	Yes	No
8. Are decisions based on data?	Yes	No
9. Has wall-to-wall planning occurred?	Yes	No
10. Have major logistical details been planned?	Yes	No
11. Is fidelity of implementation being monitored?	Yes	No
12. Is there a problem-solving plan?	Yes	No
13. Is progress information being communicated?	Yes	No
14. Is the new program integrated with existing programs?	Yes	No
15. Is staff continuity considered with new hires?	Yes	No
16. Are involved staff members supported?	Yes	No
Action Response: Using the Data		

SOURCE: Adapted with permission from Colvin, Braun, Cole, Paine, and Tobin (2006).

References

Baker, S., Gersten, R., Dimino, J. A., & Griffiths, R. (2004). The sustained use of research-based instructional practice: A case study of peer assisted learning strategies in mathematics. *Remedial and Special Education, 25*(1), 5–24.

Barton, P. E. (2005). *One-third of a nation: Rising drop-out rates and declining opportunities.* Princeton, NJ: Policy Information Center, Educational Testing Service.

Bear, G. G. (1990). Best practices in school discipline. In A. Thomas & J. Grimes (Eds.), *Best practices in school psychology–II.* (pp. 649–663). Washington, DC: National Association of School Psychologists.

Biglan, A. (1995). *Changing culture practices: A contextualistic framework for intervention research.* Reno, NV: Context Press.

Carnine, D. (1997). *How school site councils can help improve teaching and learning: A handbook for site councils and educational leaders on school improvement.* Eugene, OR: National Center to Improve the Tools of Educators, College of Education, University of Oregon.

Carnine, D. (2002). *Why education experts resist effective practices: And what it would take to make education more like medicine.* Washington, DC: Thomas B. Fordham Foundation. Available from www.edexcellence.net/library/carnine.html

Centers for Disease Control and Prevention. (2006). *National youth risk behavior survey, 1991–2005: Trends in the prevalence of behaviors that contribute to violence.* Available from www.cdc.gov/yrbss

Colvin, G. (2004). *Managing the cycle of serious acting-out behavior.* Eugene, OR: Behavior Associates.

Colvin, G., Braun, D., Cole, C., Paine, S., & Tobin, T. (2006). *Blueprint for sustaining effective programs in schools.* Eugene, OR: Bethel School District.

Colvin, G., Kame'enui, E., & Sugai, G. (1993). Reconceptualizing behavior management and school-wide discipline in general education. *Education and Treatment of Children, 16,* 361–381.

Colvin, G., & Lazar, M. (1997). *The effective elementary classroom: Managing for success.* Longmont, CO: Sopris West.

Colvin, G., & Sprick, R. (1999). Providing administrative leadership for effective behavior support: Ten strategies for principals. *Effective School Practices, 1,* 65–71.

Cotton, K. (1995). *Effective schools research summary: 1995 update.* Portland, OR: Northwest Regional Educational Laboratory.

Darch, C. B., & Kame'enui, E. J. (2003). *Instructional classroom management: A proactive approach to behavior management* (2nd ed.). Columbus, OH: Allyn & Bacon/Merrill Education.

Duhon-Sells, R. (1995). *Dealing with youth violence: What schools and communities need to know.* Bloomington, IN: National Education Service.

Evertson, C. M., Emmer, E. T., Clements, B. S., & Worsham, M. E. (1994). *Classroom management for elementary teachers* (3rd ed.). Needham Heights, MA: Allyn & Bacon.

Frase, L. (2005). Refocusing the purposes of teacher supervision. In F. E. English (Ed.), *The Sage handbook of educational leadership: Advances in theory, research and practice* (pp. 430–462). Thousand Oaks, CA: Sage.

Fullan, M. (2002). The change leader. *Educational Leadership, 59*(8), 16–21.

Fullan, M. (2003). *The moral imperative of school leadership.* Thousand Oaks, CA: Corwin Press.

Gersten, R. G., & Woodward, J. (1990). Rethinking the Regular Education Initiative: Focus on the classroom teacher. *Remedial and Special Education, 11*(3), 7–16.

Greenberg, M. T., Weissberg, R. P., Utne O'Brien, M., Zins, J. E., Fredericks, L., Resnik, H., et al. (2003). Enhancing school-based prevention and youth development through coordinated social, emotional, and academic learning. *American Psychologist, 58*, 466–474.

Grimes, J., & Tilly, D. W. (1996). Policy and process: Means to lasting educational change. *School Psychology Review, 25*, 465–476.

Guskey, T. (1986). Staff development and the process of teacher change. *Educational Researcher, 15*(5), 5–12.

Hall, D. (2005, June). *Getting honest about grad rates: How states play the numbers and students lose.* Washington, DC: Education Trust.

Hargreaves, A., & Fink, D. (2006). *Sustainable leadership.* San Francisco, CA: Jossey-Bass.

Heylighen, F., & Joslyn, C. (1992). *What is system's theory?* Retrieved December 1, 2006, from http://pespmc1.vub.ac.be/SYSTHEOR.html

Hodgkinson, H. (1998). The demographics of diversity. *Principal, 78*(1), 26–32.

Hord, S. M., Rutherford, W. L., Huling, L., & Hall, G. E. (2004). *Taking charge of change.* Austin, TX: Southwest Educational Development Laboratory.

Horner, R. H., Sugai, G., Todd, A. W., & Lewis-Palmer, T. (2005). School-wide positive behavior support: An alternative approach to discipline in schools. In L. Bambara & L. Kern (Eds.), *Individualized supports for students with problem behavior: Designing positive behavior plans* (pp. 359–390). New York: Guilford Press.

Joint Economic Committee. (1991, August). *Doing drugs and dropping out: A report prepared for the use of the subcommittee on economic growth, trade, and taxes of the Joint Economic Committee.* Washington, DC: U.S. Government Printing Office.

Jordan, W. A., Lara, J., & McPartland, J. M. (1996). Exploring the causes of early dropout among race-ethnic and gender groups. *Youth & Society, 28*, 62–94.

Kauffman, J. M., Mostert, M. P., Trent, S. C., & Hallahan, D. P. (1998). *Managing classroom behavior: A reflective case-based approach.* Needham Heights, MA: Allyn & Bacon.

Kaye, S. (1997). Education of children with disabilities. *Disability Statistics Abstract, 19*, 1–4.

Krug, E. G., Mercy, J. A., Dahlberg, L. L., & Zwi, A. B. (2002). The world report on violence and health. *Lancet, 5*(360), 1083–1088.

Latham, G. (1988). The birth and death cycles of educational innovations. *Principal, 68*(1), 41–43.

Lehr, C. A., Johnson, D. R., Bremer, C. D., Cosio, A., & Thompson, M. (2004). *Increasing rates of school completion: Moving from policy and research to practice.* Washington, DC: National Center on Secondary Education and Transition, U.S. Department of Education, Office of Special Education Programs.

Leithwood, K., Seashore Louis, K., Anderson, S., & Wahistrom, K. (2004). *Review of research: How leadership influences student learning.* New York: Wallace Foundation.

Lewis, T. J., & Sugai, G. (1999). Effective behavior support: A systems approach to proactive schoolwide management. *Focus on Exceptional Children, 31*(6), 1–24.

Luiselli, J. K., Putnam, R. F., & Sunderland, M. (2002). Longitudinal evaluation of behavior support intervention in a public middle school. *Journal of Positive Behavior Interventions, 4*, 182–188.

McNeely, C. A., Nonnemaker, J. M., & Blum, R. W. (2002). Promoting school connectedness: Evidence from a national longitudinal study of adolescent health. *Journal of School Health, 72*(4), 138–146.

National Center for Children in Poverty. (2006). *Basic facts about low-income children.* New York: Columbia University, Mailman School of Public Health.

National Center for Education Statistics. (1995). Washington, DC: U.S. Department of Education.

National Center for Education Statistics. (2002). Washington, DC: U.S. Department of Education.

National Center for Education Statistics. (2003). Washington, DC: U.S. Department of Education.

National Center for Injury Prevention and Control. (2006). *Youth violence: Fact sheet.* Atlanta, GA: Centers for Disease Control and Prevention.

Nelson, J. R., Martella, R., & Galand, B. (1998). The effects of teaching school expectations and establishing consistent consequences on formal office disciplinary actions. *Journal of Emotional and Behavioral Disorders,6*(3), 153–161.

Office of Special Education Programs, Center on Positive and Behavioral Interventions and Supports. (2004). *School-wide and behavior support implementers' blueprint and support assessment.* Eugene, OR: University of Oregon.

OSERS 23rd annual report to Congress on the implementation of the IDEA. (2001). Jessup, MD: Education Publications Center, U.S. Department of Education.

Resnick, M. D., Ireland, M., & Borowsky, I. (2004).Youth violence perpetration: What protects? What predicts? Findings from the National Longitudinal Study of Adolescent Health. *Journal of Adolescent Health, 35,* 424.e1–e10.

Rose, L. C., & Gallup, A. M. (1998). *The 30th annual Phi Delta Kappa/Gallup poll of the public's attitude towards the public schools.* Bloomington, IN: Phi Delta Kappa International.

Rose, L. C., & Gallup, A. M. (2006). *The 38th annual Phi Delta Kappa/Gallup poll of the public's attitude towards the public schools.* Bloomington, IN: Phi Delta Kappa International.

Scanlon, D., & Mellard, D. F. (2002). Academic and participation profiles of school-age dropouts with and without disabilities. *Exceptional Children, 68,* 239–258.

Simon Weinstein, C. (2003). *Secondary classroom management: Lessons from research and practice* (2nd ed.). Boston: McGraw-Hill.

Slavin, R. E. (1989, June). PET and the pendulum: Faddism in education and how to stop it. *Phi Delta Kappan, 70,* 752–758.

Smylie, M. A. (1988). The enhancement function of staff development: Organizational and psychological antecedents to individual teacher change. *American Educational Research Journal, 25,* 1–30.

Sprick, R., Garrison, M., & Howard, L. (1998). *CHAMPs: A proactive and positive approach to classroom management.* Eugene, OR: Pacific Northwest.

Sprick, R., Sprick, M., & Garrison, M. (1992). *Foundations: Developing school-wide discipline policies.* Eugene, OR: Pacific Northwest.

Sprick, R., Wise, B., Marcum, K., Haykim, M., & Howard, L. (2005). *Administrator's desk reference of behavioral management (Volumes I, II, III).* Eugene, OR: Pacific Northwest.

Sugai, G. (1996). Providing effective behavior support to all students: Procedures and processes. *Technical Assistance Journal: Oregon Special Education, 11,* 1–4.

Sugai, G., & Horner, R. H. (2002). The evolution of discipline practices: School-wide positive behavior supports. *Child and Family Behavior Therapy, 24,* 23–50.

Sugai, G., & Horner, R. (2006). A promising approach for expanding and sustaining the implementation of schoolwide positive behavior support. *School Psychology Review, 35,* 245–259.

Sugai, G., & Horner, R. (2006). A promising approach for expanding and sustaining school-wide positive behavior support. *School Psychology Review, 35,* 245–259.

Sugai, G., Kame'enui, E., & Colvin, G. (1990). *Project PREPARE: Promoting responsible, empirical and proactive alternatives in regular education for students with behavior disorders.* Eugene, OR: University of Oregon.

Todd, A., Horner, R., Sugai, G., & Colvin, G. (1999). Individualizing school-wide discipline for students with chronic problem behaviors: A team approach. *Effective School Practices, 17*(4), 72–82.

Todd, A. W., Horner, R. H., Sugai, G., & Sprague, J. R. (1999). Effective behavior support: Strengthening schoolwide systems through a team-based approach. *Effective School Practices, 17*(4), 23–27.

Togneri, W., & Anderson, E. A. (2003). *Beyond islands of excellence: What districts can do to improve instruction and achievement in all schools—a leadership brief.* Washington, DC: Learning First Alliance.

Turnbull, A., Edmonson, H., Griggs, P., Wickham, D., Freeman, R., Guess, D., et al. (2002). A blueprint for schoolwide positive behavior support: Implementation of three components. *Exceptional Children, 68,* 377–402.

U.S. Department of Justice, Bureau of Justice Statistics. (2005). *Prison statistics.* Washington, DC: Author.

Wagner, M. (1991). *Drop-outs with disabilities: What do we know? What can we do?* Menlo Park, CA: SRI International.

Wagner, M. (1995). Outcomes for youths with serious emotional disturbance in secondary schools and early adulthood. *Future of Children, 5*(2), 90–112.

Walker, H., Colvin, G., & Ramsey, E. (1995). *Antisocial behavior in school: Strategies and best practices.* Pacific Grove, CA: Brooks/Cole.

Wong, H. K., & Wong, R. T. (1991). *The first days of school: How to be an effective teacher.* Sunnyvale, CA: Harry K. Wong.

Zins, J. E., & Ponti, C. R. (1990). Best practices in school-based consultation. In A. Thomas & J. Grimes (Eds.), *Best practices in school psychology—II* (pp. 673–694). Washington, DC: National Association of School Psychologists.

Credits

This page constitutes an extension of the copyright page. Every effort has been made to trace the ownership of the copyrighted material and to secure permission from copyright holders. In the event of any issue regarding the use of material in this book, we will be pleased to make any corrections for future printings.

Thanks are due to the following authors, publishers, and agencies for permission to use the material indicated.

Chapter 2: Figure 2.1. Source: Adapted with permission from OSEP Center on Positive and Behavioral Interventions and Supports (2004). *School-Wide and Behavior Support Implementers' Blueprint and Support Assessment.* University of Oregon.

Chapter 3: Boxes 3.1–3.11. Source: From Colvin, Geoff, and Sprick, Randy, Providing administrative leadership for effective behavior support: Ten strategies for principals, *in Effective School Practices*, 1, 65–71. Copyright © 1999 by Association for Direct Instruction. Reprinted with permission.

Chapter 6: Boxes 6.2–6.4. Source: Courtesy of Anchorage School District, Anchorage, Alaska.

Chapter 10: Figures 10.1, 10.3, 10.6, 10.8, 10.9. Source: Courtesy of Anchorage School District, Anchorage, Alaska.

Figures 10.2, 10.4, 10.5, 10.7. Source: Courtesy of Educational Resource Associates.

Chapter 11: Source: From Colvin, G., Braun, D., Cole, C., Paine, S., & Tobin, T. (2006). *Blueprint for Sustaining Effective Programs in Schools.* Eugene, OR: Bethel School District. Copyright © 2006 Bethel School District. Adapted with permission.

Index

**CORWIN
PRESS**

The Corwin Press logo—a raven striding across an open book—represents the union of courage and learning. Corwin Press is committed to improving education for all learners by publishing books and other professional development resources for those serving the field of PreK–12 education. By providing practical, hands-on materials, Corwin Press continues to carry out the promise of its motto: **"Helping Educators Do Their Work Better."**